KINDLY LIGHT

KINDLY LIGHT

Meditations on Newman's Poem

GORDON S. WAKEFIELD

EPWORTH PRESS

© Gordon S. Wakefield 1984

All rights reserved. No part of this publication may be reproduced, stored in a retrieval system, or transmitted, in any form or by any means, electronic, mechanical, photocopying, recording or otherwise, without the prior permission of the publisher, Epworth Press.

7162 0394 4

*First published 1984
by Epworth Press
Room 195, 1 Central Buildings, Westminster,
London SW1*

*Typeset by Gloucester Typesetting Services
and Printed in Great Britain by
Richard Clay (The Chaucer Press) Ltd
Bungay, Suffolk*

*For Karl Britton
Philosopher and friend
who accepted this dedication
but died suddenly
as the last pages were being written*

23 July 1983

Contents

Preface	ix
Introduction	xi
1 John Henry Newman and Providence	1
2 The Darkness and the Light	13
3 Reserve, Remorse, Remembrance	25
4 Towards the Dawn	35
5 The Hinterland	47
A Sermon	61
Sources, Acknowledgments, Further Reading	68

Preface

This book would not have been written at all if the Council of the Queen's College at Birmingham had not given me study leave for the summer of 1983. I am most grateful to them and also to my colleagues for their ready co-operation. I was able to spend the Trinity term in Oxford and must thank especially the Revd Dr Kenneth Wilson, Principal of Westminster College, for providing splendid conditions in which to work (including proximity to the cricket matches), and the Chaplain, the Revd Ralph Waller, for his companionship and encouragement. The hospitality and friendship of several Oxford Colleges and their Chaplains, notably Keble and Dr Geoffrey Rowell, contributed much, not only to my enjoyment but to the necessary atmosphere for a book of this kind, while the 150th anniversary of the Oxford Movement and the celebratory Conference at Keble College in July 1983, to which I had to contribute a modest critical paper, turned me to a more detailed study of the spirituality of the Tractarians than I had previously undertaken. I had also begun the academic year 1982–1983 with a sermon before the University of Oxford in which I sought to compare the two Oxford Movements of the eighteenth and nineteenth centuries, especially with regard to their understanding of holiness. This book is a testament of many friendships both of the living and the departed. The unnamed Methodist minister who recurs is the Revd Phil. J. Fisher who died in 1961. I used some of these meditations as the basis of an ecumenical Quiet Day at St Ouen's Manor, Jersey, at Pentecost 1983, and tried out the thoughts on Providence and 'the Invisible World' at a graduates' group connected with Wesley Memorial Methodist Church, Oxford. Finally, the book has been much influenced by my editorship of *A Dictionary of Christian Spirituality* (SCM Press 1983). It may not be the little child of that enterprise, but it is a blood relation.

The Queen's College Gordon S. Wakefield
Birmingham
July 1983

Introduction

In spite of the solemn season and the Orwellian year, I believe that the most suitable subject for a Lent book in 1984 would set the Methodist conviction that 'holiness is happiness' over against the despair of these apocalyptic times, while restraining the more shallow and repellent expressions of the optimism of grace, such as the car sticker which invites one to 'Honk if you love Jesus'.

This book has not turned out quite like that. For one thing, there has been published in 1983, Helen Oppenheimer's *The Hope of Happiness* (SCM Press), which admirably fulfils this purpose; for another, I have been haunted these last few months by John Henry Newman. Many, not least some who knew him, have found him rather depressing, hardly an exemplar of cheerfulness, and his spirituality was very different from that of John Wesley and the Methodists. In his Anglican days, he and his fellow authors of *Tracts for the Times* were in part reacting against Methodism and evangelicalism, which they found over-exuberant, excited, hectically emotional. Yet the poem which is the basis of the following chapters invokes the 'kindly light' of Christ and breathes a spirit of realistic hope amid 'the encircling gloom'. And there have been and still are Methodists who have found that Newman's lines speak to their condition. Denominational differences are real and none the less so for being so often of culture and 'style' rather than theology. Over many years I have come to learn, sometimes painfully, the contrast between Methodist openness and Tractarian reserve, which recurs in these pages. But within the denominations there are people of differing temperaments to whom the spirituality associated with other Christian groups may be more congenial than that which should be native. And so I offer these meditations which draw heavily on Newman, but sometimes extend the discussion from his starting-point, to members of my own but also of other communions, with the prayer that they may find in them, not simply a 'cordial for drooping spirits', but a diet to refresh and strengthen faith in the wilderness both of Lent and of this world.

I must venture the hope that the spirituality I try to expound will point to a third way between the revived and ascendant evangelicalism of the past decade and the declining but articulate and effective radicalism, which in the Methodist Church may be seen as the alternatives for Christians today. There is a more 'mystical' spirituality, represented in Charles Wesley's hymns, and expressed in John Burnaby's *Amor Dei* (Hodder and Stoughton 1938), one of the profoundest theological works of my lifetime:

> Behind the law of Moses stands the Covenant which makes Israel God's people and Jehovah their God; beyond the Body broken on the Cross is the love wherewith the Father loved the Son before the foundation of the world, the unity into which all the friends of the Crucified are to be made perfect: *that they may be one even as we are one ... that the love where with thou lovedst me may be in them and I in them.*

For this, tradition as well as scripture is the ground (though neither uncritically received), liturgy is central and the Catholic spirit the ethos. The church is more than a number of divergent companies in the business of Christianity, which sociologists may investigate, managerial skills assist and mergers in some instances promote. It is the Body of Christ and includes not only those who may be enumerated throughout the world, but the whole company of heaven. It is more comprehensive than we have dreamed. Its philosophy is enshrined in ancient and ecumenical creeds, its faith works by love. Hidden with Christ in God it never for one moment forgets the needs of the world.

That may seem a far cry from these individualistic verses of a minor poet (though a great thinker) of the nineteenth century, which may be thought by some to be rather sentimental for our time, but I believe that it describes the true 'hinterland' of this plea from the lone pilgrim way, and that there are many who will not be borne on eagle's wings to the Mount of God, but whom the 'kindly light' will guide one step at a time to the union which is Christ's prayer for his own.

This is intended as a book of devotion rather than a work of scholarship and I have not encumbered the text with references which might prove distracting. There is a section in which I acknowledge sources, and indebtedness, and give guidance for further reading. This may be found helpful to leaders if the book is used in groups. I have not included a list of questions since it is important that such should arise spontaneously and not be my attempt to 'programme' discussion. I hope that the book may inspire prayer and not simply cerebration, though, it is an axiom of mine that the spiritual life and the intellectual life must never be sundered and that the study desk is only inches away from the prie-dieu. With this Newman would be in sympathy.

I append a sermon preached in Winchester Cathedral on 13 May 1982 at an ecumenical service to commemorate the visit to Britain of Pope John Paul II. I chose to offer some reflections on Newman's later popular poetical work *The Dream of Gerontius* and I trust that its appropriateness as a tailpiece will be obvious.

Lead, kindly Light, amid the encircling gloom
    Lead Thou me on!
The night is dark, and I am far from home;
    Lead Thou me on!
Keep Thou my feet; I do not ask to see
The distant scene: one step enough for me.

I was not ever thus, nor prayed that Thou
    Shouldst lead me on.
I loved to choose and see my path, but now
    Lead Thou me on!
I loved the garish day, and, spite of fears,
Pride ruled my will: remember not past years.

So long Thy power hath blest me, sure it still
    Will lead me on
O'er moor and fen, o'er crag and torrent, till
    The night is gone;
And with the morn those angel faces smile
Which I have loved long since, and lost awhile.

I

John Henry Newman and Providence

All is dreary till we believe, what our hearts tell us, that we are subjects of his (God's) governance; nothing is dreary, all inspires hope and trust, directly we understand that we are under his hand, and that whatever comes to us is from him, as a method of discipline and guidance. What is it to us whether the knowledge he gives us be greater or less, if it be he who gives it? What is it to us whether it be exact or vague, if he bids us trust it? What have we to care whether we are or are not given to divide substance from shadow, if he is training us heavenward by means of either?

J. H. Newman, *University Sermon*, XV, 41

From the distance of almost a century the long life of John Henry Newman (1808–90) seems to be a clear example of the workings of God's Providence. It may not have fulfilled a purpose, which, as in Cowper's hymn, ripened 'fast, unfolding every hour', but there is a harvest which is still being gathered, and Newman is as significant a person for our time as his own. When he composed 'Lead kindly light', he was on his way back to England from Mediterranean travels which had not been without their hazards. He was convinced that he had a work to do in England. A second Reformation was needed, which would turn the English church from complacency and worldliness under the control of an increasingly secular state, to an awareness of 'the church Catholic and Apostolic of which she was nothing but the local presence and organ'. He resumed one of the most alluring pulpit ministries in the whole history of English Christianity and became the subtle genius of the Oxford Movement, the revival of high churchmanship, which transformed Anglicanism. As with all great religious movements its consequences were immense but ambiguous. It has made Anglicans more arrogant, and church relations more difficult, and at its worst produced an unhealthy spirituality of the sacristy and the sanctuary, as though the kingdom of God depended on cottas and chasubles. Yet it has released social energies, offered Christ on the altar and in the streets, and sought to direct the church heavenward by pointing to those mystical realities which are contained in the profound words of St Paul, 'You have died and your life is hid with Christ in God' (Col. 3.3), and in which the sacraments make us participants.

But Newman could not remain in the English church. His departure to Rome in 1845, after long delays and much painful effort towards self-justification, devastated his friends and injured not only his cause within it, but the Church of England itself. Evangelical Protestants regarded it as a perversion. Few then or for long afterwards could believe that to become a Roman Catholic could serve the divine purpose, or be anything other than a capitulation to tyrannical superstition. For Newman himself it led to many discouragements and much pain. He found the leaders of his new church, for the most part lesser men than himself, suspicious of his loyalty, jealous of his gifts, made aggressive by fear of democracy, intellectual freedom, science, and the communion he had left. 'My superiors,' he wrote 'though they may claim my obedience, have no claim on my admiration and offer nothing for my inward trust.' An able and eloquent, if somewhat myopic Methodist, J. H. Rigg, felt that Rome had swallowed up Newman into impotence.

A later generation takes a different view. True, his success may have been, as he himself averred, through failure; but his 'second journey' mellowed him, refined his doctrine, gave more scope to his genius than the decades of disappointment and seeming neglect made apparent, and brought him to a liberality which would not have been possible in his austere Anglican days. In the Church of England, he appeared a reactionary, giving the Anglican Protestant formularies a Catholic twist, upholding the tradition of the early centuries against that of the Reformation with sophisticated arguments which could almost have proved that black was white; in the Church of Rome, secure in the certainty that he belonged to the authentic body of Christ, whatever its temporal imperfections, he developed further his Anglican understanding of the nature of faith, showed increasing 'compassion for the perplexed', and became a thinker who belongs to the church universal. He died without the sight, but he was prophetic of the reforms in the Roman Church, which have so promoted reconciliation in our time, so that there are those who call Vatican II, 'Newman's Council'.

His therefore may be shown to be a 'providential way'. The 'kindly light' led him on far beyond the immediate results of his return to England in 1833. He could not see 'the distant scene', which was far other than he would have then desired. The gloom would never wholly disperse and at times it deepened. He could have offered the verses as his prayer throughout his life. At the last, he requested that on his memorial tablet should be the words *ex umbris et imaginabis in veritatem* – 'out of the shadows and reflections into truth'.

A faith in providence derived from the life of Newman does not demand any recognition of the miraculous or the magical. In later years his breath was taken away when he discovered that he had adorned a childhood verse book with a drawing of a cross and, seemingly, a rosary. There may always have been sub-conscious Catholic influences. I myself feel that it was prophetic of my own ecumenical involvement that a Wesleyan lady should inscribe 'A General Thanksgiving' from the Book of Common Prayer in the Bible she gave me at my baptism, and that close friends of my parents should have been devout Roman Catholics. These things are I believe 'signs', but they are not supernatural, although once one begins to discuss providence the distinction between natural and supernatural is difficult to draw. What is 'natural'? When his life was despaired of in Sicily, Newman was sure that he would recover. 'I must act as if I were to die, but I think God has work for me yet.' God's providence for Newman demanded a long life for its unfolding and he was preserved from accident or incapacitating illness until his work was done. So the Christ of the Fourth Gospel talks of his 'hour', which meant a life much shorter than Newman's, though not one cut off in childhood or youth. Yet may there not have been 'mute, inglorious' Newmans, and what of those not allowed to bloom at all? We cannot in the interests of 'devotion', so-called, ignore the questions which belief in personal providence raises.

A period piece?

'A sense of Providence' was common in Western society from the sixteenth to the nineteenth centuries and into our own. Puritan spirituality, with its strong Calvinism, is dominated by it, and such a theology with its insistence that the elect are few obviously takes away some of the difficulties by removing the majority of mankind from God's providence altogether. Nor must it be forgotten that Newman was brought up as a Calvinist evangelical and converted at the age of fifteen. One of the lasting results of this was to 'make me rest in the thought of two and two only absolute and luminously self-evident beings, myself and my Creator'. But in the previous century, William Law, the non-juror, from a different tradition had counselled:

> Every man is to consider himself as a particular object of God's Providence, under the same care and protection of God as if the world had been made for him alone. It is not by chance that a man is born at such a time, of such parents and in such a place and condition.

Something of this was in the very atmosphere of the nineteenth century. And not only among orthodox Christians. It is behind 'romantic' poetry, the religious experience described in Wordsworth's *The Prelude*, and in a thinker like John Stuart Mill, or a later Victorian, Matthew Arnold.

The nagging question for us is whether a sense of personal providence is not a product of a particular time, place, period and class – the so-called and much maligned 'middle class'. Social historians and the French psycho-analyst, Jacques Lacan, have supported the theory that the development of individual self-consciousness, the 'Je' or 'I', was advanced by the manufacture of mirrors. Many of our ancestors had no idea what they looked like and the chance to see themselves must have made them more interested in their bodies and personalities. But not only the proliferation of mirrors betokened the age of individualism. Christopher Hill lists other developments: 'More rooms in better-off peasant houses, use of glass in windows (common for copy-holders and ordinary poor people only since the Civil War, Aubrey says); use of coal in grates, replacement of benches by chairs . . .' It is, however, by no means certain which was cause and which effect. It may be that the demand for mirrors was the result of a new awareness of individuality, not the other way on. Certainly there is implicit in humanity the knowledge that 'I am I' is a very different assertion from 'I am a member of the species man'. The mediaeval mystic, Meister Eckhart, said:

> That I am a man
> This I share with other men
> That I see and hear, and that I eat and drink
> Is what all animals do likewise
> But that I am I is only mine and belongs to me and nobody else.

Each individual is unique. And the game we sometimes play: 'Suppose I had been so and so, or born in a different time in a different culture, or died young', is really nonsense. I would not be myself if I had been born in any other year, or possibly even month, than I was. And the New Testament regards each individual as of incalculable value in the sight of a God who notices the sparrow's fall. 'The very hairs of your head are all numbered.' 'The Son of God loved me and gave himself for me.'

The sense that my life is providentially ordered may, as Matthew Arnold implied, be accepted by literary imagination, i.e. the ability to enter into life as it is actually lived and share the feelings of human hearts, rather than by metaphysics, i.e. a grandiose intellectual attempt to construct a system of logical explanation. But it comes with an imperative and demands unquestioning dedication. As Wordsworth wrote in *The Prelude*:

> I made no vows, but vows
> Were then made for me; bond unknown to me
> Was given, that I should be, else sinning greatly,
> A dedicated Spirit.

I am not permitted any more than Peter to glance over my shoulder at another disciple, or non-disciple, and ask 'Lord what shall this man do?' His lot may seem to be more favoured than mine; it may be very much worse – and this is the real challenge to faith; but, as

Newman wrote 'What you *know* is his (God's) dealings with *you* – what you *don't* understand is his dealings with others. Go by what you know, instead of attempting what you don't know. Interpret what you don't know by what you do.'

There is no doubt that real conviction as to divine providence is often implanted in infancy. 'It depends not on what is given but on who gives it and how.' This awesome truth has further social implications for it might be demonstrated that the sense of providence is very much the result of a middle-class upbringing, which must not be assumed to be encapsulation in suburban prosperity (as with Newman himself and, contrastingly, many of those who decry the middle classes today), but which by sobriety, thrift, Christian fidelity and a strong urge to education and social betterment, maintained itself in what used to be called 'decent poverty'. Writing from the observation of degrading poverty, one who lived during the Reformation declared 'A poor man lies under a great temptation to doubt God's Providence and care.' And this goes without saying. But is not the preaching of good news to the poor an attempt, if one dares put it so, to create a Providence for them? To help them to see that though ignored, despised, deprived by the world, they are of worth to God? This is the first step to lifting them out of their poverty, by pointing them to the spiritual wealth of God's kingdom, which may be no substitute for subsistence and elementary justice if they lack even these, but which saves them from the soul-destroying bitterness of a society locked in the values of materialism, which is where social betterment by itself may lead.

What of the world?

Does not this belief in a personal providence relegate the world to 'a vale of soul-making'? It may be possible to discern some pattern or purpose in my own life, I may believe that I am destined for a particular vocation, albeit humble and obscure, but what of the process of the centuries, the course of history through all the aeons of human struggle, pleasure, pain, getting and spending, joy, sorrow, life, death? Is that ordained by God? Is a supreme purpose being worked out across the centuries, or is time just the roaring loom on which individual lives – an infinite number but few out of all the billions – are woven into a divine pattern? Newman was notoriously not a prophet of social justice and lived through 'the hungry forties' absorbed in his own soul and the church. My old teacher, R. Newton Flew, used to quote a saying he ascribed to Newman to which he could not provide a reference, and which, even with the help of the Birmingham Oratory, I have not been able to trace, but which sounds authentic: 'God is more interested in the soul of an old apple-woman than in the rise of dynasties and fall of kings.' This has not been a fashionable sentiment among Christians for many years; and there has been increasing emphasis on the interaction between individuals and the social and political conditions of their lives.

In his Anglican days, Newman had a doctrine of history, pre- and post-Christian, which is compatible with the New Testament in that it so clearly repeats the early Christian insistence that the decisive hour had struck in Christ:

The Light and Life of men had appeared, and had suffered and had risen again; and nothing more was left to do. Earth had had its most solemn event, and seen its most august sight; and therefore it was the last time. And, hence, though time intervene between Christ's first and second coming, it is not *recognized* (as I may say) in the Gospel scheme, but is, as it were, an accident. For so it was that up to Christ's coming in the flesh, the course of things ran straight towards that end, nearing it by every step; but now, under the Gospel, that course has (if I may so speak) altered its direction, as regards His second coming, and runs, not toward the end, but along it and on the brink of it; and is at all times equally near that great event, which, did it run towards, it would at once run into. Christ, then, is ever at our doors; as near eighteen hundred years ago as now, and not nearer now than then; and not nearer when He comes than now. When He says He will come 'soon', 'soon' is not a word of time but of natural order. This present state of things, 'the present distress' as St Paul calls it, is ever *close upon* the next world and resolves itself into it. As when a man is given over, he may die at any moment yet lingers; as an implement of war may any moment explode, and must at some time; as we listen for a clock to strike, and at length it surprises us; as a crumbling arch hangs, we know not how, and is not safe to pass under; so creeps on this feeble, weary world, and, one day, before we know where we are, it will end.

Such an attempt to reconcile the immediacy of the New Testament expectation of Christ's return with the continuing course of history meets a certain mood. It could calm the restless agitation of revolutionaries, which, as every historian knows, so often causes increase in human suffering, while being ultimately powerless to do more than replace one human tyranny by another. In its ethical consequences it might make common cause with Buddhism and its teaching of compassion. But it ignores such progress as there has been, as Christian values have, slowly and imperfectly, and never irreversibly, influenced civilizations. It leaves no place for the sheer wonder and excitement of scientific discovery, which, though arrogant and idolatrous, and applied for the ends of human selfishness, has been a thinking of God's thoughts after him, and to some extent his surrender in divine self-emptying of his own prerogatives to men and women for their freedom and benison. Are we to assume that this is outside the divine providence altogether since the coming of Christ? And are we simply to be passive before the horror of the world, worse almost than Newman would have dreamed of? 'Liberation Theology' is an amalgam of the Bible and Karl Marx, and open to question both by the Catholic faith and the Jesus of History. Yet the cross, as A. E. Housman saw, was the result of Jesus being unable to 'let ill alone'. Where Newman's words have weight is in their reminder that this world is 'passing away' – a truth as scientific as it is Christian, that unless we act in expectation of Christ's coming we may simply confuse Christianity with the values of the age and that God's providential order is seen once for all in the life, death and resurrection of Jesus.

'Almighty God'?

Since Newman, Christians have become less certain of the divine omnipotence, and less happy with the great forces of nature as its analogues. The Lord is not in the earthquake, the wind, the fire, or the nuclear explosion. Natural calamities, or wars, are not seen simply as his judgments. As Auden wrote in his poem 'Friday's Child', commemorating Bonhoeffer, he leaves 'the bigger bangs to us'. But the Christian, like the Bible, must hold together belief in personal providence with belief in a divine good purpose for the planet as a whole; a purpose which God does not achieve by fiat of his almighty power against which his people are infinitely rebellious and therefore made infinitely to suffer, but by his own sacrifice, his pouring out of himself in unremitting love, so that, in spite of the decisive victory of the cross, Christ will be in agony until the end of the world. The providences of our lives are to enable us to have part in 'love's endeavour, love's expense' manifested perfectly in Christ and beside which all else, however strong in big battalions of good or evil, is transient.

Irony

No understanding of providence today can reckon without the irony which is so well-known a characteristic of St John's Gospel, and which is a concept which seems necessary to the interpretation of God's dealings with us in a world like this. Reality is so different from appearance. To the world, the death of Jesus is shame, disgrace, agony, utter defeat. To faith it is the finishing of the work of the divine love; parallel to that of first creation. Jesus is judged by Pilate; but in truth, Pilate is judged by Christ. Caiaphas conspires Christ's death as an expedient in order to save the people from public disturbance and the loss of many lives. In truth, he dies for the whole world's eternal salvation. Jesus is the Resurrection and the Life, yet he who raises Lazarus in proof, must himself die as the direct consequence of that act, because only so will eternal life, far beyond the restoration of Lazarus to his family and friends in this world, be made available to those who believe.

Hiddenness

This is an aspect of the hiddenness of God which was so much a part of Newman's teaching and that of the Oxford Movement, as we shall see. The divine ways are not simple and clear to be read off nature and experience or even the Christian 'revelation' as easily as from a book. All is not sure and seen in this life. We are profoundly ignorant, because of the limitations of our own minds, but also because there is so much that we are not told. The New Testament records are woefully incomplete and lacking in detail. Newman was as aware of this as the most sceptical modern critic. The evidences of Christ's divinity were not given to the world.

> The Annunciation was secret; the Nativity was secret; the miraculous fasting in the wilderness was secret; the Resurrection secret; the Ascension not far from secret; the abiding Presence secret. One thing alone was public and in the eyes of the world – His Death; the only event which did not speak of His Divinity, the only event in which He seemed a sign not of power but of weakness.

So Newman. And he would maintain that this is all of God's mercy. It is in order that we may come to real faith, which is no mere 'notional assent', intellectual affirmation, but the total possession of our whole being and its actions by Christ. Problems, difficulties, seemingly inadequate evidence lead us on gradually *ex umbris et imaginabus in veritatem*. They also demand that we must be forever going back over the partial revelation and discerning within it fresh meaning.

This has its parallels outside Christian faith. It could be behind A. N. Whitehead's dictum that the whole of Western philosophy is a series of footnotes to Plato. Literary scholars find fresh meanings in Shakespeare in each generation. So should Christians in Holy Scripture and the Holy Tradition of the Fathers and the Creeds.

But the truth of faith, which is so much more than knowledge or information, yields itself up not to intellectual enquiry alone, nor to pious, uncritical devotion alone, but to the clear mind, following conscience and purified by humble, dedicated love, in a spirit of worship.

Thus we are committed to a journey with many hardships and struggles, 'o'er moor, o'er fen, o'er crag and torrent'. But we shall be emboldened to persist in it if we believe that we are not the victims of blind chance, or of some sporting President of the Immortals, but the servants of a love which would make us partakers of the divine life, though by sharing a strength made perfect in weakness and which seeks not our good alone but the bringing of the universe into a unity in Christ.

2

The Darkness and the Light

Some travel on in a covert, cloudy day and get home by it, have so much light as to know their way and yet do not at all clearly see the bright and full sunshine of assurance; others have it breaking forth ever and anon under a cloud; and some have it more constantly. But as all meet in the end, so all agree in the beginning, that is, in the reality of the thing.

Robert Leighton (1611–84)

By meditation we detect in Revelation this remarkable principle, which is not openly propounded, *that religious light is intellectual darkness*. As if our gracious Lord had said to us: 'Scripture does not aim at making mysteries, but they are as shadows brought out by the Sun of Truth. When you knew nothing of revealed light, you knew not revealed darkness. Religious truth requires you should be told *something*; your own imperfect nature prevents you knowing *all*; and to know *something* and *not all* – partial knowledge – must, of course, perplex; doctrines imperfectly revealed must be mysterious.'

J. H. Newman, *Parochial and Plain Sermons*, i, 211

The story of how Newman came to compose 'Lead, kindly light' is well known. On the voyage home from his Italian and Sicilian tour, in 1833, during which he had caught typhoid and nearly died, the ship was becalmed for a whole week in the strait of Bonifacio between Sardinia and Corsica. At night out of the darkness, there must have been visible one solitary light, and Newman saw it as a sign of the divine guidance, which was leading him on through many perils to the joy of morning. The poem's first published title was 'Faith-Heavenly Leadings' (1834). Two years later, it was included in *Lyra Apostolica* under the motto 'Unto the godly there ariseth up light in the darkness'. In 1868, in his *Occasional Verses*, Newman called it, 'The Pillar of the Cloud', derived from the wilderness wanderings of old Israel. 'And the Lord went before them by day in a pillar of cloud, to lead them by the way; and by night in a pillar of fire, to give them light; that they might go by day and by night' (Ex. 13.21). It thus has a link with the hymn by Charles Wesley with which the Methodist Conference habitually concludes, though Newman is individualistic; Wesley corporate.

> Captain of Israel's host and guide
> Of all who seek the land above,
> Beneath thy shadow we abide
> The cloud of thy protecting love.

Christians live in different states of light and darkness, as the quotation from the Scottish Bishop, Robert Leighton, a forgotten writer who impressed Coleridge, and some Methodist preachers, says. This is a matter of temperament, humanly speaking, or of God's way with the soul, to put it theologically. Newman belongs to Leighton's first group: 'Some travel on in a covert, cloudy day and get home by it, have so much light as to know their way and yet do not at all clearly see the bright and full sunshine of assurance.'

'The encircling gloom'

Leighton was not referring to what, in Western mystical experience has been called 'the dark night of the soul', after the sixteenth-century Spanish Carmelite, St John of the Cross; nor did Newman undergo it. His copy of the works of St John remained uncut, nor was he a student of those whom we have come to call the English Mystics, notably the anonymous author of *The Cloud of Unknowing*, who in so many ways anticipates St John. Newman was not a contemplative in the sense in which a person's prayer passes from meditation, an activity of the mind and its faculties, reason, the power to order and classify, imagination and the like, into a wordless, imageless 'regard' for God, which may lead to remarkable sights for the cleansed and purified vision, but often at the cost of a long journey through darkness and desertion, until the soul enters the divine radiancy with 'nothing between'.

Part of Newman's genius was that of a preacher, and, for the preacher, the heart of prayer is meditation, for this is what a sermon should be, an orderly product of the mind, disciplined and clear whatever its fervour and emotion, and leading to a resolution. Owen Chadwick has deftly described his spirituality:

> Those who saw Newman at the Sacrament were conscious that he was much with God. But he prayed in his own way. He had a lively mind and could not usually rest in long silences. He needed a lot of material for his prayers, a lot of thinking about Biblical texts, or devotional authors. The mode was unusual. He thought best with pen and paper, and prayer was no exception. He formed sentences, drafted poetic aspirations, and channelled his mind to express a facet of faith or hope. The devotional books which he

used were seldom classics. Almost anything served, especially if it were given him by a friend. We might expect such a man to enjoy prayer. But this was so only at moments; he suffered easily from feelings of aridity, and found prayer more often a duty than a pleasure. And he suspected that pleasure might bring with it less useful feelings, like pride in devotion, or excitement, or a sense of abnormality; whereas prayer ought to be normal, sober, quiet, calm. Newman was no man for wordless silence, or sudden outbreaks of emotion.

Such a person may know intellectual doubt, or clinical depression, but not 'the dark night of the soul', which is a severe test of faith along the contemplative way, though it may have a Protestant and non-mystical counterpart in the *angst* (anxiety, dread) of a Martin Luther, who after untold spiritual sufferings comes at last to learn that justification, our acceptance by God and standing with him is by faith alone. The contemplative learns that God is never more with us than when he seems to forsake us; and that at the last we receive the reward of the Beatific Vision because we love him not for his benefits but himself.

This was not Newman's experience; neither is it for most of us. 'The encircling gloom' was the darkness which surrounded his sensitive being, a darkness compounded of the inability of the intellect, in spite of its powers, which later Newman was to celebrate almost lyrically, to penetrate the mystery of God, and of his own sin. But he was never hopeless. In the despairing delirium of his Sicilian illness, he had comforted himself with the thought that he had not run counter to advice he had been given by men of faith, and repeated to himself 'I have not sinned against light'.

'The kindly light'

'*Kindly* light' is noteworthy. It is reminiscent of the *Phos hilaron* of the late second-century hymn which John Keble, Newman's friend and fellow-Tractarian, translated, the gladdening, gladsome light which is Christ.

> Hail gladdening light of his pure glory poured,
> Who is the immortal Father, heavenly blest.

But it is a subdued light, almost 'the candle of the Lord' in the Authorized Version of Proverbs 20.27, which meant so much to the Cambridge Platonists, seventeenth-century Anglican Divines, in whom the early Tractarians showed some interest. Newman stands as a rebuke to all superficial optimism, the misleading assurance of the revivalist hymn:

> Not a shadow can rise,
> Not a cloud in the skies,
> But his smile drives it quickly away;
> Not a doubt nor a fear,
> Not a sigh nor a tear,
> Can abide while we trust and obey.

This is deplorable, the prostitution of evangelical Christianity; and Newman's contemporary Anglican convert to the Roman Church, F. W. Faber, is not much better, in what is a banal conclusion to a good hymn:

> If our love were but more simple,
> We should take him at his word,
> And our lives would be all sunshine
> In the sweetness of our Lord.

There are those – mystics of a kind – who at some moments are able to see all life and nature transfigured by 'the light that never was on sea or land'. Thomas Traherne, a seventeenth-century Anglican, saw the corn in the fields at harvest as 'orient and immortal wheat', and the boys and girls playing in the streets as moving jewels. Charles Raven, a twentieth-century theologian, who was dedicated to the reconciliation of science and religion, had in his young manhood visions of God in the beauties of the Lakeland hills and, more remarkably, beheld the divine glory when passing a squalid fish and chip shop in a Liverpool slum, the whole scene lit, not with naphtha flares but with the Shekinah as the proprietor and his wife seemed to be distributing a sacrament. The Risen Christ was once for him undeniably experienced in the mean lodgings of a sick friend in a then depressed district of the Potteries. We may label this 'Wordsworthian', and no more than Wordsworth's sense of providence is it peculiarly Christian, though often Christ is the light; and the very mention of the poet, whom Keble admired and regarded as a master, and Newman too, reminds us that he never recovered his bright vision of the glory in nature after his brother had been drowned in the fury of the sea.

But there are those who see a greater light which streams from the cross and resurrection of Christ; not from the Creator alone, but from the Redeemer with whom Christians believe he is one. Paul would hardly describe as a 'kindly light' the blinding, felling flash of the Damascus Road.

This is not so for all. Not every Christian is destined to be a Paul and even he may not have lived in unbroken radiance, though he did write, in what Newman regarded as his most beautiful letter, of our being transfigured into the divine likeness and changed from glory to glory (II Cor. 3.18). But we do not know what Paul's end was, or whether, like Christ himself, according to St Mark, he may not have died in deepest darkness.

Be that as it may, for most of us who are aware of the distress of nations and the rampage of evil everywhere, as well as our own uncertainties and doubts, the service of *Tenebrae* is an appropriate symbol. This is a twelfth-century name given to the Matins and Lauds of the last three days of Holy Week. It means 'darkness', since over the centuries, the morning offices tended to be pushed back to the evening of the previous day to save people rising very early. As the offices proceeded, all the lights (candles) would be extinguished save one representing Christ, who alone shines out against the darkness of seemingly victorious evil.

> Lead kindly Light, amid the encircling gloom,
>   Lead Thou me on!

'The candle of the Lord'

It is worth pausing on the thought of candlelight. Modern versions of Proverbs 20.27 do not give the same sense as that which the Cambridge Platonists knew and made the foundation of their theology – 'The spirit of man is the candle of the Lord'. The Revised Standard Version prefers 'lamp', but the New English Bible changes the whole meaning: 'The Lord shines into a man's very soul searching out his inmost being.' The older expositors believed that there was a light of God in every human being, lit by him, his 'prevenient grace', and illumining what otherwise would be gross darkness, and although at times but a feeble flicker, leading to God's truth.

Candlelight is very different from the sun. Yet it reveals beauty more enchantingly and, I suppose, sensuously, though with an alluring delicacy and restraint. It deepens mystery. A Lincolnshire shepherd was once shown into the chapel of Bishop Edward King and he noticed that there were two candles on the altar, which many at that time (*c.* 1890) would have regarded as signs of a Romeward tendency. The shepherd reacted otherwise. 'I see, Sir, that yours is a yon-side religion,' he said.

Candlelight is 'kindly', gentle. There is no harsh glare. It does not expose or enlarge. At the end of Dietrich Bonhoeffer's *Ethics*, there is a footnote which reproduces a letter of 1943, telling among other things, how some friends of his had watched a film of the life of a plant in quick motion. They were horrified. They felt it was an obscene intrusion into private mystery.

Our world is not satisfied with candlelight. It must bring everything into view, before the floodlights; all must be seen and seen through. There is no restraint and in the end we may be left with a world of nothingness, without humanity or beauty, a black void into which no good can come, but in which evil and suspicion lurk.

The light God gives is more like a candle than a searchlight. It leaves much hidden. This, as we have already observed, was a conviction of Newman's. It demands the response of reverence.

'Discerning the mystery'

An eighteenth-century work was entitled 'Christianity not mysterious'. It dealt in rational theology, and although the so-called 'enlightenment' often brought a cold rather than a kindly light, we may be grateful for what a historian has deemed 'the abiding distinction of the West' that it has gone further in the last three hundred years than any other society the world has ever known to rid itself of the cruel fears and superstitions expressed in witchcraft, magic and Devil worship.

The trouble is that the triumph of the rational and scientific spirit has been two-edged, both destructive. On the one hand there has been a sterilization with the real danger of a computer civilization which, as the same historian has said, leaves no place 'for the emotions, including the finer ones of love and compassion, or for the sense of aesthetic mystery and wonder which is at the root of all great literature, art and music'. Transubstantiation *may* be bad eucharistic theology. It is innocent compared with the use made of scientific discoveries and the conditioning of human nature by their ruthless 'behaviourist' and other applications. On the other hand there is an alarming revival and globe-encircling spread of magical beliefs and customs, and the cults which Anthony Burgess has exposed with such ruthless brilliance in his novels *The Clockwork Orange* and *Earthly Powers*.

Only the Christian religion, in spite of its own periodic capitulations to the spirit of evil, is capable of accommodating the human need for mystery, wonder and worship with the affirmation that perfect love casts out fear – perfect love, not simply right reason.

The word mystery belongs to the New Testament as well as to the mystery religions which were youthful Christianity's contemporaries. But the Christian mystery is a secret hidden throughout the ages but revealed in Christ – God's universal love for humanity beyond his chosen people. This is revealed not in teaching, but in the death of God's Son. And here indeed, as Charles Wesley declares, is mystery:

> Tis mystery all! The immortal dies
> Who can explore his strange design?
> In vain the first-born seraph tries
> To sound the depths of love divine
> Tis mercy all! Let earth adore!
> Let angel minds enquire no more!

The change in the penultimate line is very significant. 'Tis mystery all! ... Tis *mercy* all'. That is the wonder of the eternal God that he in his infinite goodness, his absolute perfection, shows mercy to sinners – to *me*.

The danger is that this may be cheapened. Isaac Williams, another of the Tractarian circle around Newman, felt that Methodists and evangelicals profaned the atonement by their raucous shouting at street corners and their roof-raising hymns about those events which shook the earth and veiled the sun. What was worse, there was a real sense in which conversion through the preaching of the cross became a matter of feelings, of excitement and 'experience' rather than a real change of heart and allegiance. For Paul the preaching of Christ crucified meant 'the necessity of our being crucified to the world'. It was a more awesome event than a change from dissipation to respectability.

Newman could never easily be familiar with God or with the stupendous demands of holiness. This was what made him, like Williams, unhappy with evangelicals:

> ... what I shrink from is their rudeness, irreverence and almost profaneness; the profaneness of making a most sacred doctrine a subject of vehement declaration, or instrument of exciting the feelings, or topic for vague, general reiterated statement in technical language. Surely this feeling of mine need not arise from mere fastidiousness of education – it ought to exist in everyone. The poorest and humblest ought to shrink from the lightness and hardness with which a certain school speaks of the adorable work and sufferings of our Saviour. Zaccheus, unrefined as he was, did not intrude himself on our Lord – the woman that was a sinner silently bedewed his feet.

Newman believed that the Christian mystery was to be taught in worship rather than in words. Bishop Butler's ethical sermons were sparing in their references to Christian doctrine, but he put up a cross in his private chapel and was charged with popery. It is an intriguing thought that our real testimony may be in the way we worship, how we engage in what we may be inclined to think are the externals of religion. Newman himself always by his whole manner and personality communicated a sense of 'the awfulness of things unseen'. 'There was something *sui generis* in the profoundly serious, profoundly reverent tone, about everything that touched religion'.

The kindly light leads us to the light which is unapproachable. It does not dissolve the mystery; it draws us into it, with 'subdued, chastened, trembling joy'. And the mystery is of the divine love, the love of the Father for the Son in the Holy Spirit. This we discern as there is awakened in our hearts a 'sense of wondering awe, which is the light in which we see light'.

'Treasures of darkness'

In these realms Christian language becomes paradoxical. Said Newman in a youthful sermon, delivered when he was but twenty-eight years of age, 'Religious light is intellectual darkness.' Not that he ever disparaged the intellect, though because he was such an intellectual he mistrusted it, especially when he was young. Twenty-five years later in his treatise on education, *The Idea of a University*, he hymned it in some fine passages. It is no mere machine for the processing of knowledge handed down; nor is it just a storehouse of information; it is a living force which compares, classifies, comprehends, infers and interrogates experience. 'It is the clear, calm accurate vision of all things as far as the finite mind can embrace them.' It has proportion, clarity, calm and something of 'the repose of faith'. 'It has almost the beauty of heavenly contemplation, so intimate is it with the eternal order of things and the music of the spheres.' Yet it cannot subdue the pride and passion of man. Mind is all-glorious, yet forever insufficient. God alone can save us.

Education cannot do what religion alone provides, the union of response to 'the moral law within', conscience, duty, and to the ineffable mystery which requires metaphors of darkness rather than of light. 'God is light and in him is no darkness at all', yet 'clouds and darkness are round about him'. He 'clothes himself with light as with a garment', and a garment conceals nakedness, even though it expresses personality. Mystics have spoken paradoxically of the 'ray of darkness'. As the Greek Fathers were fond of stressing, Moses went into the cloud to meet God, and there is a knowledge possible only there.

St John of the Cross describes with sublime lyricism the especial glories of the night: he may be thinking not only of his spiritual experience but of the darkness of the night which covered him when he escaped from prison in Toledo, while he is not afraid to use of his union with God the especial raptures which the passionate intimacy of the night gives to human lovers:

> O night that led my eyes,
> O darkness better loved than morning skies,
> O night that clasped the lover
> To his bride, each of them transfigured
> Into ecstasies such as love all lovers unifies

Elsewhere, St John says that the 'dark night of the soul' is in fact the divine light assailing it. The light causes the darkness; 'for not only does it overcome it, but likewise it overwhelms it and darkens the act of its natural intelligence'.

We must not find here too close a parallel with Newman for, as we have already explained, he was no Western mystic, and much more influenced by the early Fathers than the later tradition and, for him, the darkness was more that of doubt and the impossibility of certain intellectual proof of God and his truth. But he finds a mercy in all this. The last stanza of Henry Vaughan's poem 'Night' would be echoed in his experience:

> There is in God, some say,
> A deep but dazzling darkness, as men here

> Say it is late and dusky, because they
>   See not all clear
> O for that night! where I in him
> Might live invisible and dim.

Protestants, too, have their conviction that there are 'treasures of darkness', though they find these not through mystical journeys, or the transcendence of the intellect, so much as in the experiences of living, the things which happen to us in human relations and the course of the world. Many would say that they have learned more of the love of God through suffering and pain than through all the hours of unremitting happiness.

That last is a sentence which one may write almost glibly. It is a statement of what is declared so often that it could be the convention of a terrible insincerity. Some suffering is not like a cloud through which we see every now and then gleams of a promised glory and which brings us into the nearer presence of God; it is as a door barred and bolted against which we beat in vain, and which shuts us in forever. Such suffering as I have seen and known has not by God's mercy destroyed my faith as yet, or made me less conscious of his reality, but I am not sure that I have found him within it, so much as believed that it could not separate me – or other sufferers – from the love manifest in the darkness of Calvary. Perhaps that is the same thing. I know I take great comfort from faith in a God to whom the darkness and the light are both alike and for whom the night shines as the day.

3

Reserve, Remorse, Remembrance

His marvellous providence works beneath a veil, which speaks but an untrue language; and to see Him who is the Truth and the Life, we must stoop underneath it, and so in our turn hide ourselves from the world. They who present themselves at kings' courts, pass on to the inner chambers, where the gaze of the rude multitude cannot pierce; and we, if we would see the King of kings in His glory, must be content to disappear from the things that are seen. Hid are the saints of God . . .
>   J. H. Newman, *Parochial and Plain Sermons*, ii, 9

>   Nature withdraws from human sight
>   The treasures of her light,
>   In earth's deep mines, or ocean's cells,
>   Her secret glory dwells.
>   'Tis darkly thro' night's veil on high
>   She shews the starry sky;
>   And where of beauty ought is found,
>   She draws a shade around;
>   Nor fully e'er unveils to sense
>   Steps of bright Providence.
>   Isaac Williams, *The Cathedral*

>   Time's waters will not ebb, nor stay
>   Power cannot change them, but Love may
>   What cannot be, Love counts it done.
>   John Keble, *The Christian Year*

'I was not ever thus.' Newman, like all of us, had guilt feelings, though not, it would seem, to do with sex. 'Pride ruled my will.' He longed to make plans and achieve them. He wanted to accomplish, to be recognized, to be lauded for his own sake. 'I loved the garish day.' The 'kindly light' was not enough.

For one thing, he wanted to be able to see the future and plan a course to a successful goal. This may not seem immoral or sinful but it has received the warnings of spiritual counsellors. The Puritan John Howe (1630–1705) has an appendix to his study *Thoughtfulness for the Morrow* called 'Concerning the Immoderate Desire of Foreknowing Things to Come'. Such desire betokens lack of faith in God's providence and may result in all-consuming ambition regardless of other people, and also in an inability to live in the present, to lose 'the sacrament of the present moment and all its graces'. True, we need to be able to look forward. In trouble it helps to keep us buoyant and hopeful; in times of happiness it is as well, without inhibiting our joy or making us mistrustful of God's good gifts, or failing to share wholeheartedly in 'laughter and the love of friends', to be undergirded by a sober realism that we cannot escape our share of the world's pain, and that our faith may yet be tested almost to breaking point. Ignatius Loyola, founder of the Jesuits, with the amazing psychological insight which suffuses the *Spiritual Exercises* and his delicacy of feeling for the states of those who put themselves under the discipline of the regime he prescribes, wrote in his 'Rules for the Discernment of Spirits': 'Let him who is in consolation think how it will be with him in the desolation which will follow, laying up fresh strength for that time.'

But it is not precisely here that the worst danger lies; rather, in 'wishing one's life away' by not concentrating on the present, allowing the mind to flit to the next engagement when in the midst of some taxing interview, or when gardening, or playing with one's children; or not being content with one's present lot, wanting some better thing, more eminent position, greater fame. This eye on 'the distant scene', even if it be only the near distance, robs one not only of the proper performance of one's duties in the present, but of much joy and satisfaction by the way. How many parents are left wishing that their children could be young again, not simply because of the inveterate and illusory belief that we would do better next time, or out of forgetfulness of the restrictions and annoyances children impose, but because we did not enjoy as we ought what God had given us, since we were always planning ahead, or even more likely, distracted by our own concerns and ambitions. As age advances it is even more necessary to our soul's health to live in the present, which is all we have, to savour each experience, even if it be not unmixed with anxiety and sorrow, to turn each moment to God and our chief end, which is also our beginning and our now.

'The garish day' and the need of 'reserve'

Newman himself wanted to shine or, in our modern colloquialism, to have the spotlight always on him. This is a severe temptation for many people, especially those with gifts which are likely to bring them into public view. It takes us to a direct consideration of the principle or doctrine of 'reserve', which is so necessary to an understanding of the Oxford Movement in its beginnings and first leaders. It has almost been the refrain of what we have said so far about the hiddenness of God's providence, the contrast between the kindly light and the full blaze of assurance, the need of reverence before the mystery of the divine love, and the fact that God may be found more truly in the darkness than in the light. It was the subject of two of the tracts by which the Oxford Anglicans campaigned, numbers 80 and 87, written by Isaac Williams, and it constantly recurs in

Keble, while in various forms it pervades Newman's work throughout his life.

The Tractarians discovered it in the early Fathers, who found it necessary to practice an arcane or secret discipline whereby the most solemn acts and profoundest truths of Christianity were concealed not only from a hostile and unbelieving world, but from those in preparation for baptism. The meaning of the sacraments themselves as well as the high doctrines of the faith were not disclosed until after initiation. This also seems to have been a characteristic of the ministry of Christ himself, who told many things by parables, not to make them plain or perspicuous by anecdote but to reveal them only to those who would accept and tease them out by faith and action. There is no blinding revelation of truth, but 'if any man willeth to do his will, he shall know of the doctrine'. Jesus kept his messiahship secret and was not anxious during his ministry to have either the nature of his vocation, or his mighty works, blazoned abroad. After the resurrection he showed himself to his disciples and not to the world. The last the world saw of him was when his body was taken down from the cross and sealed in the tomb. And this must be the temper of Christian discipleship.

It means that our primary aim in all that we do will be God's glory, to 'serve with a single-heart and eye', and that any praise or encouragement or self-satisfaction we receive will be a gift from him. So many of us love to display our peacock's feathers and though it may be innocent and endearing it could lead to a self-absorption which vitiates our testimony and finally imprisons us in ourselves, making us incapable of communion with God or with other people. John Keble when select preacher at Oxford once preached a University sermon which so overwhelmed his friends Newman and Froude that they walked back to their college in silence and it was some time before they could trust themselves to speak. Keble got to hear of this and deliberately turned his sermon the next week into a tedious and inconsequential harangue so that he should not receive the glory due to God alone. That is extreme and was not perhaps what God required. Yet it should make those of us who exult in our numinous passages and lilting periods uneasy and restrain not only our showmanship but our lust for praise. When I was very young, and pleased because people seemed to be liking my sermons, I told one of my Methodist spiritual guides with some delight and he answered 'Whenever anyone compliments you after a service, always make an immediate inward offering to God.'

It is not only the preacher who needs to practise a certain reserve, to flee the garish day. There are those who wish always to dominate and to be the cynosure. There is also the matter of manipulation, to use a modern cliché. This has become a 'dirty word'. It is in some ways inevitable in human relations. We often need to pray – to our fellows as well as to God – and to persuade, on behalf of others and not only for ourselves. This becomes an evil when we use unfair or deceitful methods, or when we are seeking a power which is not ours to have, wishing to assert ourselves, to dominate, to control at the expense of others and perhaps even in God's place. In all this there must be a self-surrender, and a desire to be delivered from the 'I, me, mine and the like' in which *Theologia Germanica* finds the root of Adam's sin.

We ought probably to be more reserved in our self-disclosure. Certainly we ought not always to be talking about ourselves, our interests, achievements, our troubles, much less our dedication. As Newman said '. . . the true life is a hidden life in the heart; and though it cannot exist without deeds, yet these are for the most part secret deeds, secret charities, secret prayers, secret self-denials, secret struggles, secret victories'.

Some of us are too 'open'. I was once rebuked in my youth for a 'too trusting nature'. What may have been innocence with regard to other people was a combination of pride or carelessness in myself, a jaunty, rather bouncing self-satisfaction, a belief that all the world was as interested in me as I was in myself, and a fundamental lack of discipline. I am not sure that I have overcome any of these faults, though I may have been so enabled to come to terms with the realities of life as to have been granted a diminished sense of my own importance. I know that many of us need to learn true shyness – a reserve about ourselves combined with an unselfconscious openness towards others. The modern world does not encourage this, the cult of personality, the immediate and easy use of Christian names. One of the casualties may be friendship which is in peril of being made impossible by sex-obsessed prurience, but also by the too easy and immediate familiarity, which does not wait for gradual discovery or permit growth in intimacy and true love. The rendering void of sometimes fussy and snobbish distinctions may be baneful if all become familiars and none friends.

A corollary of this is the avoidance of indiscretion, of careless talk, of gossip which betrays confidences. Preachers in the Free Church tradition have been inclined not only to illustrate too much from the first person, but to use the experiences of those who have been in their pastoral care. This may have the noblest intentions and be of great help to their hearers. It may make the minister of Christ into a novelist. This may be his gift, but it places him in a moral dilemma, as indeed it does the secular writer of fiction. One is aghast to realize how closely the characters of an Evelyn Waugh or a C. P. Snow are drawn from real people, some of whom one has known oneself. There are precedents in the Christian classics. Bunyan's characters must have been types of real life – they are not just vivid icons. William Law's engaging sketches in *A Serious Call* must have been based on actual *exempla*. Sometimes people are much helped when they recognize themselves in what the preacher says or the spiritual guide writes. But there must be delicacy, restraint, caution, reserve. And the evangelical or the humanist Christian may need to go to school with the Fathers and the Tractarians. Not least those traditions which practise the confessional and its seal are of value here.

The persistence of sin

'I was not ever thus,' says Newman at thirty-two years of age, abandoned to the divine providence, content to live a life of humble trust in God, not asserting his own will or serving his own ambition, hidden from the glare of the world.

Newman believed that his sins went back a long way. 'Past years' are not those of his manhood alone. He did not think that childhood was a stage of goodness and innocence before 'shades of the prison house' began to close. He admired Wordsworth's 'Ode on the Intimations of Immortality in Early Childhood' and once read it aloud most beautifully to a friend in his Roman Catholic years. He also believed that a child's mind is naturally poetic and age and knowledge change it to prose. But in his Anglican days at any rate he believed that infants commit sins which affect them all their lives, and in several places, as one expositor puts it, 'refers to the extent to which men and women, by the hardly noticed imprudences and failures of their youth, bind on their backs burdens which press them almost to the ground in later life'. There is a famous reminiscence which classes Newman with Augustine, Richard Baxter and others. His father, brother and himself rode over to a friend's house from Norwood in south London where they lived,

> and the gardener gave us three apricots – and my father telling me to choose, I took the largest, a thing which still distresses me whenever I think of it.

He could not regard this as a peccadillo. It was a sign of his propensity to disobey his conscience even when young. I myself cannot idealize childhood. I am conscious of all my adult weaknesses from an age long before puberty. My sins have grown up with me. The worst things I have done or thought in manhood were incipient when I was a boy; and some cruelties manhood has repressed.

What is more disturbing is that in spite of his dedication and resolve when he wrote 'Lead, kindly light', Newman was still reproaching himself for the same faults ten years afterwards at Littlemore: '. . . that my motive in all my exertions during the last ten years has been the pleasure of energizing intellectually as if my talents were given me to play a game with . . . that self-love in one shape or another, e.g. vanity, desire of the good opinion of friends, etc. have been my motive, and that possibly is *the* sovereign sin in my heart'.

Do we ever really change? Do we not in spite of our motions towards God and goodness, even possibly a dramatic conversion which revolutionizes our whole way of life, remain the same people, with the same inveterate weaknesses and sins which are transposed into a different key? This could be demonstrated from the famous instances of Paul, Augustine, Luther and Wesley. Paul, as a Christian, was very much what he had been before in his nervous passion and vehemence and proneness at times to cruelty. And it could be argued that in the others there are still traces of their innate sins.

Yet there is no need for pessimism. We have to recognize that God does not 'force' the soul. Its spiritual development is a growth which takes time. No one is made perfect at a clap, in Bunyan's phrase. The providential way is not a straight path, it is winding, devious, uphill, with many diversions and strewn with broken resolutions. There must be persistence in spite of failure, perpetual penitence, an increasingly tender conscience and the faith that God is leading us on. What is important about conversion is that it is a change of allegiance and environment. We need to be in the *milieu* in which we can grow into the divine likeness. This does not inevitably mean that 'the lines will fall in pleasant places'. Many are refined in the fire, which may not be persecutions or concentration camps, but discouragements and failures such as Newman endured, or that many of us discover in the ordinary relations, struggles and sufferings of what may seem sheltered lives. The church will be no perpetual delight in the communion of saints. It will often be as it was for Newman an engagement with folk of limited imagination, whose views we do not share, and indeed to whose understanding of the faith we may be profoundly opposed. Yet there is no salvation outside. And they must endure us as we them. Only we must hope that we are on the right road. And we must not brood on past sins, or be forever returning to our failures. 'Remember not past years' is Newman's prayer to God; it is also good advice to himself.

The place of memory

Yet is it possible? Do we not have to live with memory, our own, other people's and God's? Is it possible for the past to be erased from the mind without the total death of the individuals within it? And should we be the same persons unless we both remembered and were remembered? (This, incidentally, is an argument against re-incarnation. If I have no memory of a previous existence, how can I be the same person?)

This is as disturbing as it is comforting. Whenever Peter is thought of, the story of his denial of Jesus is brought to mind. He carries the church's memory of that to all eternity, as well as his own.

Yet memory is one of the most beneficent faculties of the human *psyche*. This is not because it heals through distance making possible a perhaps lazy reluctance to re-engage in 'old, unhappy far-off things and battles long ago'; but because it changes the meaning of the past, and perhaps thereby changes the past itself. E. M. Forster pointed out that the title of Marcel Proust's novel, which he regarded as second only to Tolstoy's *War and Peace* is not *Things Past* but *Remembrance of Things Past*. 'What really matters in the book is not the events but the remembering of events.' 'It reconsiders the same episode, the same characters and reaches new results. It keeps turning the stuff of life about, and looking through it from this direction and that.' Some interpreters of Proust have said that memory delivers us from the ephemeral, the pointless, sets free the permanent essence of things, enables discernment not only of their successiveness but of their simultaneity as they are seen from the eternal vantage-point. So, as Richard Hooker eloquently affirms in the final words of his sermon on justification, Peter, chastened, but restored, would see a greater strength and blessing in his tears of humiliation and penitence than in all his brave protestations of fidelity, and, we may add, in his later achievements, which all flowed from his failure and forgiveness. And memory sees such glory in the cross of Christ, in history and in itself an instrument of most brutal torture, total shame and utter degradation, that a mediaevel poet dared say:

> O felix culpa! O happy fault
> To merit this Redeemer.

In the end we do not want God to forget but to remember us in his

Son. Thus the past is transformed by his mercy and, as we make the memorial of Christ before God, we have the promise of our transfiguration from glory to glory.

> Look, Father, Look on his anointed face,
> And only look on us as found in him.

4

Towards the Dawn

In No Strange Land

'The kingdom of God is within you'

O world invisible, we view thee,
O world intangible, we touch thee,
O world unknowable, we know thee,
Inapprehensible, we clutch thee!

Does the fish soar to find the ocean,
The eagle plunge to find the air –
That we ask of the stars in motion
If they have rumour of thee there?

Not where the wheeling systems darken,
And our benumbed conceiving soars! –
The drift of pinions would we hearken,
Beats at our own clay-shuttered doors.

The angels keep their ancient places; –
Turn but a stone and start a wing!
'Tis ye, 'tis your estranged faces,
That miss the many-splendoured thing.

But (when so sad thou canst not sadder)
Cry; – and upon thy so sore loss
Shall shine the traffic of Jacob's ladder
Pitched between heaven and Charing Cross.

Yea, in the night, my Soul, my daughter,
Cry, – clinging heaven by the hems;
And lo, Christ walking on the water,
Not of Gennesareth, but Thames!

          Francis Thompson (1859–1907)

In a sermon preached in the summer of 1948, at Westminster Central Hall, the Methodist W. E. Sangster dramatically contrasted the early Methodists with Newman. 'They did not sing "Lead, kindly light amid the encircling gloom", but My God, I *know*, I feel thee mine.' Newman's 'sober trust' and somewhat nervous caution are pallid and depressing beside the exuberant certainties of the Methodist tradition.

Sangster was right, in that Newman, at any rate as an Anglican, denied absolutely that the individual could be certain of salvation. This he held in common with all the Tractarians, who believed that the Christian life began and continued in holy fear. 'There is no safety, brethren, but never to think ourselves safe.' So Pusey. For Newman much of this cringing from assurance goes back to the Calvinism of his youth, which fixed forever in his mind the stern warning of Jesus that 'many are called, few chosen', and also caused him to react sharply in later life from its belief that the elect could know that they were among the saved. He contrasts this self-confidence with Paul's ascetic discipline, 'lest I myself should become a castaway', and he finds the temper of the assured utterly obnoxious:

> Now, if a man thinks he knows for certain that he shall be saved, of course he will be much tempted to indulge in a carnal security, and to look down upon others, and that, whether the true flock of Christ is large or small. It is not the knowledge that the chosen are *few* which occasions these bad feelings, but a man's private assurance that *he* is chosen.

Methodism with its assertion of free will and its universalism believed that it was possible to fall from grace and therefore there should be no relaxation from the disciplines of love:

> Lest that my fearful case should be,
> Each moment knit my soul to thee;
> And lead me to the mount above
> Through the low vale of humble love.

But along with this, there was a conviction, based on Romans 8.14–17 that there is an 'inward witness' of God's own Spirit reinforcing the certainty of our own hearts that we are the children of God. Wesley himself interpreted this in a very rational way, even devising a syllogism of assurance and laying down most emphatically that we could be certain of our adoption only if we were bringing forth the fruit of good works. Holiness, love, was the test. Newman would feel that even this was rather dangerous and laid the believer open to self-deceit and pride, while the fervent, enthusiastic atmosphere of Methodist meetings, though probably not so far removed from the early Christian worship which lay behind Paul's passage, was totally alien to his own sensitive nature. And for him 'the witness of the Spirit' reinforcing his own conscience, which would never be sufficient to give him certainty, was the witness of the church which was the Spirit's home, of its whole life of worship and of creed.

Newman, the intellectual who was suspicious of the intellect, was also the individualist, who mistrusted himself. He found assurance not in some knowledge personally imparted to his own heart, but in the institutional church, and he became convinced that the Church of Rome 'answered to the church of the first ages . . . both in substantial holiness and in actual descent'. He remained sure of this in spite of all his discouragements and disillusionments in the Roman obedience. He believed in all the church's outward signs from the Pope and the apostolic order of ministry to relics and, above all, in the real Presence of Christ in the sacrament of the altar. 'I am writing in the next room to the Chapel,' he says in an early Roman Catholic letter. 'It is such an incomprehensible blessing to have Christ's bodily presence in one's house, within one's walls, as swallows up all other privileges and destroys, or should destroy, every pain. To know that he is close by – to be able again and again through the day to go into him.' This is what gave him assurance such as he could not receive by 'inward witness'. It may seem to us incredible, we may even feel that it cannot withstand the investigations of either history or philosophy and is far removed from the religion of the New Testament. We ourselves may find our assurance in scripture or personal experience. But this was Newman's peace as it has been for millions. And we may follow his spiritual pilgrimage from what a Baptist scholar has called 'the pathetic pleading of "Lead, kindly light" to the triumphant confidence of *The Dream of Gerontius*', Yet even the former is not devoid of assurance, though quietly expressed:

> So long Thy power hath blest me, *sure* it still
>   Will lead me on

The angels and the world invisible

Since the poem became a hymn, it has been much used at funerals, though less in recent years than in the first half of this century. Its popularity in times of bereavement has been due to what I feel to be a misunderstanding – the identification of the 'angel faces' with our departed friends. Christians do not believe that the redeemed become angels, who are a different order of being, though the matter is somewhat confused, since in scripture the term 'holy ones' is used interchangeably for saints and angels, and in Mark 12.25 and parallels Jesus says, 'When they rise from the dead they neither marry nor are given in marriage but are as angels in heaven.'

Newman thought of angels as the powers of the invisible world which his pride and self-will had made less real to him. He once said that he wished he lived in the unseen world as he thought he did not live in this. He confesses that as a child 'I thought life might be a dream and I an angel, and all this world a deception, my fellow angels, by a playful device, concealing themselves from me, and deceiving me with the semblance of a material world.' This may not be so very different from his boyhood interest in magical powers and talismans and wishing 'the Arabian tales' were true. But this sense of the reality of things unseen remained powerful when he became a man.

In one of his most anthologized sermons, on 'The Invisible World' he said: 'In spite of this universal world which we see, there is another world quite as far spreading, quite as close to us and more wonderful; another world all around us though we see it not, and more wonderful than the world we see if only for this reason if for no other that we do not see it.' 'We are then in a world of spirits, as well as in a world of sense, and we hold communion with it, and take part in it, though we are not conscious of doing so.' Worship is to give us a glimpse of this invisible world. 'The ordinances we behold force the unseen truth upon our senses.'

This is the world of the angels. At one time, Newman thought that to talk of laws of nature and pursue philosophical explanations of phenomena was a slighting of the angels and an ascription to other forces of what is really their work. 'Those events which we ascribe to chance as the weather, or to nature as the seasons, are duties done to God who maketh his angels to be winds and his ministers a flame of fire ... Every breath of air and ray of light and heat, every beautiful prospect is, as it were, the skirts of their garments, the waving of the robes of those whose faces see God in heaven ...' We may be inclined to exclaim 'O that it were so!'; but this is, I fear, lovely nonsense and could almost be as absurd as the effusions of the young woman in Wodehouse, who thought of the stars as God's daisy chain, though it is a romantic affirmation of the reality of the spiritual universe. Francis Thompson, a Roman Catholic poet, was later to write a poem 'In No Strange Land', in which he too proclaims the reality and the proximity of the invisible world. 'The kingdom of God is within you' ... 'Turn but a stone and start a wing' ... 'the traffic of Jacob's ladder Pitched between heaven and Charing Cross'. Newman later ceased to believe in the idea of an angelic office in nature and reconciled more closely his intellectual and religious ideas, but he continued to believe in angels. In *The Dream of Gerontius*, the subject has a guardian angel, who, after death, bears him to the throne of God and thereafter commits him to the merciful and cleansing sleep of purgatory. There is a chorus of 'angelicals' who incessantly praise God, and also the angel, who strengthened Christ in his agony in the garden, pleading for the soul. Charles Wesley found angelic ministrations among the riches God bestows through the love of Jesus:

> Angels our servants are,
> And keep in all our ways
> And in their watchful hands they bear
> The sacred sons of grace.

Modern scientific man is not impressed – some women perhaps more so. The Methodist Sunday Service of 1975 excludes angels from the eucharistic prayer as a concession to the twentieth-century mood. No longer do Methodists praise God with angels and archangels as in other rites but simply with all the company of heaven. And it must be confessed that few worshippers seem to have noticed the omission. I am not aware of any protests.

Angels have sometimes been associated with a world view which is palpably false. The legend of their appearance at the Battle of Mons in the First World War was sign of an illusion both dangerous and pathetic. And some mystical souls may inhabit a world of the imagination so that they never engage with sensible realities. The gospel becomes a fairy-tale removed from what Sir Edwyn Hoskyns used to call 'rough, crude history'. Christ 'took on him not the nature of angels but the seed of Abraham'. There is a Victorian Christmas carol, much-loved because of its proclamation of peace, but based on a curious and certainly unbiblical cyclic view of history, which is entirely about the angels and Bethlehem and their song, but with no mention of the birth of the child, who is our peace:

> It came upon the midnight clear
> That glorious song of old
> Of angels bending near the earth,
> To touch their harps of gold.

> Peace on the earth, goodwill to men
> From heaven's Almighty King
> The world in solemn stillness lay
> To hear the angels sing.

There is nostalgia and the poignant, tragic longing of mankind for peace; but it is not the Christmas gospel, which is not of a sight and song of angels but of the Word made flesh. And Christ died on the cross with no legions of angels to rescue him and wrought our redemption in his naked, unprotected body.

Christian devotion, Protestant as much as Catholic, has sometimes need to call in the angels because our highest praises are so feeble and unworthy to celebrate the glory of God. 'Angels assist our mighty joys!' (Watts). 'Angels help us to adore him' (Lyte). And Jacob's ladder has been seen as a great symbol of Christian spirituality. The angels going up and down are the figures of the commerce between earth and heaven, the messengers of God. But according to the interpretation of the Fourth Evangelist, derived from the fact that the Hebrew word for ladder is masculine and therefore Genesis 28.12 could be translated 'the angels of God ascending and descending upon *him*', the ladder is Christ, the Son of Man. He 'gathers into one things earthly and heavenly'. In John Climacus' *The Ladder of Divine Ascent*, a seventh-century work of great influence in Eastern spirituality, which has comparatively few references to the ladder of Jacob's dream, love is what he sees at the summit, and the condition of the angels is that of love. It is interesting that in the hymn by the American Methodist, Frances Jane van Alstyne (1820–1915), which sings of 'Blessed assurance, Jesus is mine' in a way which might well have repelled Newman, one of the phenomena of the state, along with 'perfect delight' and 'visions of rapture' is 'angels descending' to bring 'echoes of mercy, whispers of love'. It is a revivalist lyric not intended for theological analysis, any more than Newman's poem for which he refused in his old age to provide an interpretation, but the angels are so to speak brought in to enhance the sense of almost delirious joy. Yet it is as well to recall Walter Hilton, the English mystic's implicit rebuke of his contemporary Richard Rolle for whom angels' songs were almost the supreme joy of the beatific state. They are, says Hilton, but a secondary light. God is our all in all.

There have been those in our materialistic and scientifically conditioned age who have detected a need for the recovery of faith in the supernatural. This was well argued in a book published at the end of the 1960s by Peter Berger and intriguingly called *A Rumour of Angels*. It was not a study of angelology, or a plea for a Newmanesque belief in such beings, but a winsome, though very serious argument from human experience, tragedy and evil, as well as joy and goodness, for the recognition of a world beyond this.

Many of a scientific training recoil from an implicit dualism. Not only do they dismiss as superstition anything not susceptible of rigorous empirical verification, they are convinced that this is a *uni*verse, a whole. There is nothing *super*natural above or beyond nature and, ultimately, investigation by science.

But there is no need to go beyond normal human experience to endorse the long tradition, deriving from Plato, and republished in the Franciscan Bonaventura and many others, that 'two world's are ours'. Sir Thomas Browne (1606–82), the Norwich physician, wrote in *Religio Medici*:

> ... thus is man that great and true *Amphibium*, whose nature is disposed to live not onely like other creatures in divers elements, but in divided and distinguished worlds; for though there bee but one (world) to sense, there are two to reason; the one visible; the other invisible ...

This, however, raises two great problems, one metaphysical, the other moral. First, does the invisible world, the world within, of thought, imagination, memory, which so transcends the limitations of time and space, correspond to any objective reality outside myself? Is there a spiritual universe where all our private inner worlds intersect, where there is possible meeting in the spirit? This surely must be so and one does not need to invoke the telepathic and the psychic to try to prove it. We inhabit an objective, invisible world through common culture, common tradition of literature and music, common prayer, though here it has to be recognized that this invisible world is divided into as many continents as the earth.

The second and moral problem is that the other world is not necessarily good. Evil is not simply of the earth, earthy. There are, as the New Testament recognizes so well, spiritual forces of wickedness in the heavenly places from which indeed the sin of this world comes. And for many the spiritual world is hell; they do not leave the cares and troubles and limitations of the temporal for the peace and joy of heaven but for a world filled with the hideous shapes of lust and death, a mental prison. Demons rather than angels are its inhabitants.

It is here that we light upon the wonder and comfort of the Christian gospel, which begins not with the worlds, but with Christ. He, as we have already said, 'gathers into one things earthly and heavenly' and his victory is above all over the 'principalities and powers' of the other world, so that the torments of the imagination, the hell within our own selves, are overcome by what God did once for all in him.

It is the Fourth Evangelist whose cosmology is most satisfying in a scientific age, for the Jesus who talks with his disciples, who eats and drinks and knows joy and sorrow in this world, leaves physical and temporal existence for the Father's house, which is not another universe but an enlargement of this. He goes on ahead to make ready for his disciples a dwelling in a sphere which is not discontinuous with the life they are already living while still not taken out of this world. Their relation with the Lord who is risen and ascended takes its character from his circumstances not from theirs. Thus 'while it is impossible to place Heaven in the world, it is impossible not to place the world in Heaven ... Jesus Christ, then, lives in the same world with us and we in the same Heaven with him, and it is in what passes between him and us that our salvation lies.'

Newman's poem contains the implicit and terrible warning that we may lose 'the angel faces', the sense of spiritual realities, or, to put it in the terms to which our musings have led us, our co-existence with Christ. It is said that Charles Darwin, after years of concentration on his researches, lost his capacity for music and poetry and the arts. Newman thought that he had lost his vision through pride, self-determination, a desire to plot his own course, choose and see his own path. This led him away from luminous reality. It could be that, as with Darwin, our problem is not moral, simply that the world is too much with us and not in its evil, but in preoccupations within it which dull the imagination and make disclosures of the divine impossible. But God is merciful, and although we need to train and use our spiritual senses, and, if we are Christians, never to neglect worship and prayer, which are our hold on things unseen, he has a way of confronting us when we least expect him in realities very much of this world, a child born in a stable, or a man dying on a cross for love, which things 'angels long to see into'.

5

The Hinterland

One alone is constant; One alone is true to us; One alone can be true; One alone can be all things to us; One alone can supply our needs; One alone can train us up to our full perfection; One alone can give a meaning to our complex and intricate nature; One alone can give us tune and harmony; One alone can form and possess. Are we allowed to put ourselves under His guidance? This surely is the only question.

J. H. Newman, *Parochial and Plain Sermons*, v, 326

Men look upon religion as a rigid and austere thing that comes to rob them of their joy, they must never have a smile more, they must never have a summer day after it, but thou canst tell them of the sweetness and deliciousness that is in the ways of grace, thou canst assure them that all the ways of wisdom are pleasantness; thou canst assure them that grace does not mean to take away their joy, but only to refine it, that it does not mean to put out the light, but only to snuff it, that it may burn brighter and clearer . . . spiritual joy, 'tis the most clarified joy, aye and & 'tis solid and massy joy, beaten joy, like beaten gold.

Nicholas Culverwell (1654), *The White Stone*, 133

The poem is personal, subjective, part of an individual's autobiography and it is strange that it should have been sung as a hymn. But, apart from the misunderstanding of the angel faces, the poem became popular, because, as Owen Chadwick says: 'The Victorian generation found itself in this language. Unsure about the Bible, afraid of Marx and class-war, agonized by evolution and the hostility of nature, hesitant over its moral foundations, struggling with slums and exploitation – later Victorians heard Newman's stanzas, made them their own and voiced their own hesitant act of faith.' It has always spoken to the personal condition of some: Cosmo Lang, a future Archbishop of Canterbury, who joined in the singing of it in Cuddesdon Parish Church at the end of the service to which he dedicated himself to seek the priestly vocation; a Methodist minister known to me in my earlier years, twenty years Lang's junior, who 'proved' the second verse in a ministry of outstanding gifts, with his providential way full of ironies, and recognition largely denied him; and in our own day and from a different sphere, the 'cellist, Julian Lloyd Webber.

To try to expose its meaning we have had to go far beyond the text. This is a poem of personal faith; there is nothing of the objectivity of the church's creed about it. If it is a hymn for congregational worship at all, it is to borrow a distinction of J. E. Rattenbury's applied to Wesley, a hymn of the pilgrim way, not of the great hinterland of Catholic Christianity.

What must we affirm, if we are to allow it to lead us to fullness of faith and practice? To state this will help us to gather up some of the foregoing thoughts.

1. The supreme revelation of God is in Jesus Christ and what happened to him – his life, death and their sequel, which Christians have believed was his vindication in the eternal order.

This is the key to the meaning of history and to our own individual lives. It is not easy to believe this because it all took place a long time ago, and while the outline of Christ's life is clear and indisputable, there is a disturbing lack or uncertainty of detail, and much depends on the interpretation of rather scanty facts by the first followers of Jesus and the church since. We have to trust the tradition, though we may be more rigorous than Newman in feeling that some of the developments are not a genuine growth from the original seed which fell into the ground and died. But ultimately we have to trust the witnesses throughout the ages, and to proceed by a 'philosophy of "as if"'. Believe, behave, 'as if' the gospel were true and you will find it validated.

Newman adduced the Virgin Mary as the pattern of faith, because she continued to ponder in her heart what she had first accepted on trust.

> She does not think it enough to accept, she dwells upon it; not enough to possess, she uses it; not enough to assent, she develops it; not indeed reasoning first, and believing afterwards, with Zacharias, yet first believing without reasoning, next from love and reverence, reasoning after believing.

It is remarkable how open we may be on many details of faith, which, as we ponder and reason them out over the years, become more credible as we see their place in the Christian scheme. Take the belief that thirty-six hours after his death and burial, the tomb of Jesus was found empty. This is an early tradition, though it does not seem to have been known to St Paul, since his evidences of the resurrection in I Corinthians 15 all concern the appearances of Jesus to his disciples. It may well be that the gospel of the resurrection was preached in some places without the story of the empty tomb, and it has to be admitted that if Christ's body had disappeared from the place where it was known to have been laid, it is strange that the enemies of Jesus did not produce a body from somewhere to try and scotch rumours. Yet the tradition of the empty tomb, though conveyed in stories which have some elements of legend, the appearance of angels and the like, makes assertions of such magnitude that the more one meditates, the more one wonders if it is not demanded by faith in a God, whose salvation includes not only the spiritual but the material world. It may be one of the details which are not essential to the credal affirmation 'the third day he rose from the dead', yet which the life of faith makes more not less credible.

What is essential is to see the unity of the 'things concerning Jesus'. In his Anglican days, Newman was in some danger of falling into the ancient heresy, which so stresses Christ's Godhead that he is hardly a real man. This is a grave error, though one totally uncongenial to our time. What it asserts is important, that the significance of Jesus is in his relation to God and that this life, obscure by some standards, and ending in apparent failure, discloses the true nature and activity of the One who set this whole universe in motion and is the paradigm of God's dealings with the human race throughout the ages. This has never been stated better than by Newman's contemporary, Robert Browning, in the poem 'A Death in the Desert', in which the aged and dying author of the Fourth Gospel gives his final testimony:

> Is not God now i' the world His power first made?
> Is not His love at issue still with sin
> Visibly when a wrong is done on earth?
> Love, wrong and pain, what see I else around?
> Yea, and the Resurrection and Uprise
> To the right hand of the throne – what is it beside,
> When such truth breaking bounds, o'erfloods my soul,
> And, as I saw the sin and death, even so
> See I the need yet transiency of both,
> The good and glory consummated thence?

This governs belief in Providence. God's leading of me, the ordering of my steps, is not to make me prosperous or famed or successful, but that I may fulfil in my own life his purposes in Christ; that the 'Christ-event' may be repeated in me – changes of period and culture apart... If I am uniquely called, it is that I may share in his passion and progress to the Father for the life of the world. In my own circumstances, I must die to live, find my life by losing it, and love must be the meaning both of my actions, and of what I have to accept through those things over which I have little or no control. I must not be over-dramatic in all this, cast myself ostentatiously in the role of Christ, make it add to my own self-importance. This is where 'reserve' is so necessary, and Newman's words already quoted should be ploughed into our souls:

> ... the true life is a hidden life in the heart; and though it cannot exist without deeds, yet these are for the most part secret deeds, secret charities, secret prayers, secret self-denials, secret struggles, secret victories.

John Keble's morning hymn states what should be the case for most of us:

> The trivial round, the common task
> Will furnish all we ought to ask,
> Room to deny ourselves, a road
> To bring us daily nearer God.

2. I am a unique person, myself and no one else, and my course is solitary. Herein lies the glory and the tragedy of every human soul. Pascal, the seventeenth-century Frenchman, who has much in common with the nineteenth-century Dane, Kierkegaard, and who was not without influence on the Oxford Movement, declared in memorable words: 'The last act is always tragedy... We die alone.' And yet it is also true that, 'I am never less alone than when alone.' Not only am I involved in all mankind, not only is friendship a source of sublime joy and inspiration, but my incorporation into Christ means that my companions are not confined to those visibly around me, they include the whole company of heaven.

What shall sustain our faith (under God's grace) when we try to adhere to the Ancient Truth and seem solitary? What shall nerve the 'watchman on the walls of Jerusalem' against the scorn and jealousy of the world, the charge of singularity, of fancifulness, of extravagance, of rashness? What shall keep us calm and peaceful within, when accused of 'troubling Israel' and 'prophesying evil'? What but the vision of the Saints of all ages, whose steps we follow? What but the image of Christ mystical stamped upon our hearts and memories? ... We are not solitary; ... those multitudes in the primitive time, who believed, and taught, and worshipped, as we do, still live unto God, and ... cry from the Altar.

In Newman's spirituality, 'Lead, kindly light' is completed by *The Dream of Gerontius*. There the dying man is seen on his way to God by a whole host of friends, living and departed, and by an innumerable company of angels.

3. Liturgy is central to the whole Christian life. The Tractarians inherited a church in which the holy communion was not celebrated very frequently in most places. John Wesley in the Methodist Revival had found it to be a 'converting' as well as a 'confirming' ordinance, and seems to have been in favour of the restoration of what he believed to be the primitive practice of 'the daily sacrifice'. But this was a revivalist manifestation, and perhaps for that reason could not change the custom of the church at large, while the separation of the Wesleyan Methodist Connexion from the Church of England after Wesley's death, not in any way schismatic, resulted in a reluctance to set up rival Methodist tables, and an encouragement to Methodists to communicate in their parish churches. The Oxford Fathers succeeded in turning into Anglican practice the faith of the Wesley eucharistic hymns, though not in the Wesleyan spirit, for they would not be at home in the crowded enthusiasm of Wesley's services, just as they might share some reservations about the parish communion movement today. Newman, at St Mary's, introduced weekly celebrations, but at an early hour. 'We shall remember how we got up early in the morning, and how all things, light or darkness, sun or air, cold or freshness, breathed of Him – of Him the Lord of Glory, who stood over us, and came down upon us, and gave himself to us.'

In his early enthusiasm as a Roman Catholic, Newman found the Mass the centre and focus of his religion:

> To me nothing is so consoling, so piercing, so thrilling, so overcoming as the Mass ... It is not a mere form of words – it is a great action, the greatest action that can be on earth. It is, not the invocation merely, but, if I dare use the word, the evocation of the Eternal. He becomes present on the altar in flesh and blood, before whom angels bow and devils tremble ... There are little children there, and old men, and simple labourers, and students in seminaries ... there are innocent maidens and there are penitents; but out of these many minds rises one eucharistic hymn, and the great Action is the measure and the scope of it.

One does not need to affirm the doctrine of the Council of Trent to which Newman gives expression to share his joy and wonder in the eucharist. The Orthodox belief, as expounded by Alexander Schmemann, rings truer to many in our day, that the liturgy is our weekly journey into the kingdom of God, the life of the age to come, from which we return to the work and worship of time, inspired and strengthened by the mysteries we have shared and by the food we have received from the heavenly banquet.

The richness of the eucharist is inexhaustible, for it contains the whole of the gospel and shows forth the Christian life. It is our participation in the Son's offering of himself to the Father in love and obedience. And although our share in the eucharistic action involves every faculty of our being, not least the mind and understanding, and should be the supreme opportunity of contemplation, it is, as Newman saw, *action* in which we are engaged, Christ's and ours; it is not simply a matter of concepts or ideas. We express by worship what is beyond all words, and rites and ceremonies teach truth more than does direct explanation ... That is why hymn-singing is so vital a part of Free Church worship. Said R. W. Dale, who was minister at Carrs Lane, Birmingham, while Newman was at the Oratory: 'Let me write the hymns and I do not care who writes the theology.' When we are not following prescribed orders, our hymns are our liturgy, reaching deeper than the merely intelligible.

Liturgy is not something we make up, nor is it something that can be simply 'understood': it is something we participate in not just as minds, but with all that we are – body and soul. Hence the importance in liturgy of gestures and movement, of the sequence of the seasons through which time itself is sanctified. The liturgy unfolds the varied significance of the mystery of Christ and the fact that it cannot all be explained, the fact that much that we do, we do simply because we have always done it, conveys a rich sense of the unfathomableness of the Christian mystery.

As a corollary of this, music and words are not merely accompaniments or settings, or 'vehicles of communication'. You cannot produce poetry by inviting a poet to find words, images or rhythms for certain ideas; nor are prayers composed that way; nor the music of the Mass. There must be an inspiration which is not imprisoned or earth bound by the clamours for intelligibility, or the desire to set everyone jigging and jiving.

Liturgy may be thought of as a 'storage-system' of the great Christian images. It keeps, locked deep in its vaults, the whole of the Christian gospel, the totality of scripture, and the continuing experience of the ages. If we were exposed to the whole of this at once we might be overwhelmed into impotence; but out of its treasure things new and old are brought a little at a time so that every now and then we are confronted with certain half-forgotten demands of the teaching of Christ or his apostles, or with the sheer wonder of God's mighty acts. 'Say what you will there is something *astonishing* about the Christian religion,' says Pascal; and again, 'On our knees we need to remember the deep abysses of judgment and mercy on which the foundations of our prayers are laid.'

This may indeed strike home to one who has no Christian roots, in church or out of it, and God is certainly not confined to his ordinances. But the regular assistant at the liturgy may sometimes find that truth shines with a brilliance such as changes his whole life, as when Antony heard the words of the story of the rich young ruler: 'If thou wouldst be perfect, go sell all thou hast and give to the poor, and come, follow me.' He took them as a command to him. He obeyed and became the pioneer of the movement towards the monastic life.

I myself was once at a Cathedral eucharist. I had been worshipping there regularly for some weeks. The Gospel for the day was being intoned – a style to which as a Methodist I am not accustomed, and which in some moods I might deprecate as archaic and artificial if not displeasing to God. On this occasion the Gospel was the Parable of the Great Feast, and the final words struck me with an awesome power as never before: 'For I say unto you, That none of those men that were bidden shall taste of my supper.'

They would not have had that effect, which will remain with me for the rest of my days, if they had been part of a service devised to convert people, or if they had been read in a normal voice, either in the casual and flat style of a lector with no poetry in his soul, or with the histrionics of one who felt them too passionately.

4. The light is 'kindly', cheering. 'Holiness is happiness' is Wesley not Newman, who in his earlier years favoured a slogan taught him by a fine evangelical – 'Holiness rather than peace'. On lesser lips, Wesley's may be a shallow maxim not without a tincture of callousness. Yet our world is so full of gloomy forebodings and misery that there is almost a Christian duty of happiness. Newman was aware of this in his day:

> Gloom is no Christian temper; that repentance is not real which has not love in it; that self-chastisement is not acceptable, which is not sweetened by faith and cheerfulness. We must live in sunshine, even when we sorrow; we must live in God's presence, we must not shut ourselves up in our own hearts, even when we are reckoning up our past sins.

Prophecies of doom are often self-fulfilling. They do not avert calamity or relieve distress but help to engender the mood of hopelessness in which the dire forecasts prove true. They may be self-indulgent. Owen Chadwick has written of Ernest Renan's ability 'to enjoy philosophic despair'. And there have always been those in the church who take delight in making other people feel guilty and uncomfortable, and who utter their Jeremiads from a sense of great superiority 'Thank God I am not as those naive and cheerful fools; I am sensitive to the condition of the world and know the danger we are in.'

This is not to ignore the note of judgment in the gospel, which is more awful than those who nag and denounce conceive. But there is something suburban about depression – which is not to deny its reality or justification. Sometimes those in the worst circumstances display a cheerful courage, which at once shames and inspires those of us with a modicum of security, and, by 'southern' standards, affluence. I heard of a Peruvian priest in a shanty-town in the wake of a landslide, which had destroyed many homes. His church was a miserable shack. He found it somehow inspiring that the midnight Mass of the Nativity had been celebrated in conditions worse than those of the first Christmas.

All that we have so far dwelt on in this chapter are aids to Christian cheerfulness. First, the gospel itself, good out of evil, life out of death, the love of God from which nothing can separate us and, behind all, the knowledge that this is no fairy-tale refusal to accept the tragedy of the world, or to pretend that those who trust in Christ will have an easy path with speedy deliverance from all their troubles; that there is no 'encircling gloom'. Then there is friendship.

> In the communion of the saints,
> Is wisdom, safety and delight
> And when my heart declines and faints,
> 'Tis raiséd by their heat and light.

And worship, too, recalls perpetually the mystery of God's love, and enables us to share it as we are caught up into his kingdom and survey our lives and our world in the vast proportions of eternity.

But the cheerfulness of Christians is in God himself. An old writer, under the name of Denys the Areopagite, says that the divine ecstasy made the worlds. Our terrible century has outlawed the doctrine of the divine impassibility, the classic belief that God in his perfection does not suffer but is all joy. The Studdert-Kennedys have denounced it, the martyr Dietrich Bonhoeffer declared from his Nazi prison, 'Only a suffering God can help', the process philosopher, A. N. Whitehead, described God as 'the great companion, the fellow-sufferer who understands'. And the doctrine of the divine impassibility has received what from the biblical theologians of a former generation, who still have their successors in the liberation theologians, was the extreme of opprobrium – it represents the contamination of the gospel by Hellenism, it is Greek not Hebrew.

Julian of Norwich, a great teacher of cheerfulness, would agree with Bonhoeffer from her anchoress's cell and her own very different sufferings. But she would expound her 'showings' of a bleeding Saviour in terms of the most impeccable Trinitarian orthodoxy. 'All the Trinity worked in Christ's Passion, administering abundant virtues and plentiful grace to us by him; but only the Virgin's Son suffered, in which all the blessed Trinity rejoice.' And she reconciles the truth of Pascal's saying that Christ will be in agony until the end of the world with faith in his finished work and final victory, through her understanding of the church. 'For insofar as Christ is our head, he is glorious and impassible; but with respect to his body, to which all his members are joined, he is not fully glorified, nor wholly impassible.'

We need to recover the understanding of the divine joy, which was never better expressed than by Peter Sterry, in seventeenth-century England, who bridged the gap between the Puritans and the Cambridge Platonists and was a harbinger of the spirit of reconciliation. He wrote:

> Abide in the Father's love by spiritual joy. Joy is love flaming. One saith that laughter is the dance of the spirits, their freest motion in harmony, and that the light of the heavens is the laughter of angels. Spiritual joy is the laughter of the Divine love, of the Eternal Spirit which is in our spirits.

There is much more like this in writers with Puritan affinities than is popularly supposed. They affirm joy at the heart of the Godhead, joy in the presence of the angels of God, and, not least, as in the verse of a song for primary children: 'God is glad when we are glad.'

Earlier this century, the Roman Catholic lay theologian, Baron von Hügel, wrote an essay on 'Suffering and God', in which he restated the orthodoxy which Lady Julian expounds, and defended the doctrine of the divine impassibility, by a distinction between suffering and sympathy, which is hard to sustain linguistically, since sympathy means 'suffering with'. But his argument ought not to be dismissed:

> Let us be wise and sober, and rest satisfied with that deep Sympathy in God and this deep Suffering in Christ. Let us be satisfied, not only because this, and not more than this, appears to be the truth, but because we thus keep secure the only quite wholesome, the only sufficiently deep, outlook for our own utilisation – the outlook for which the Ultimate Intention, as indeed already the First Cause of all things, is not Sin or Suffering or Want, but Delectation, Joy and Holiness.

The essay ends with an anecdote from his own personal experience. One Good Friday forenoon in Rome, he had overslept and was too late for any of the services. The church doors were all locked against him, and, disconsolate, he turned into a new and ugly park in the Villa Borghese and sat wearily in the hot sun, his back against one of the young, shadeless trees. The only life around was in frisking green lizards.

All his wretchedness and despair closed in upon him; 'that mass of failures, disappointments, pettinesses' which was Friedrich von Hügel. (And note that from outward view many would regard him as a privileged person with an enviable lot.) His self-despair articulated itself into 'special grievances and antipathies' against 'Churchmen and Agnostics, Jews and Protestants', even his friends.

And then, suddenly, all changed. He saw as it were in procession all those who had ennobled the eternal city of Rome by their goodness and self-sacrifice. Not only Christians and martyrs, but pagans and philosophers. 'And all of them were marked by Suffering – and more or less marred by Sin.'

> But, then behind and above all these, appeared the Master of Masters, Suffering Love, gently, pathetically triumphant – Jesus Christ, Our Lord, on this day of His utter Passion. And yet,

somehow, even this, especially this utter woe, this day of that woe, they seem best expressed just simply as Good – as 'Good' Friday . . .

'Somehow here the intense Suffering led on to Joy – to the infinite Good that had sprung from this infinite Sorrow. And then came the final state of soul and outlook: God, God in Himself.' And here, in contrast even with the human Jesus, appeared pure Joy, 'an Ocean of it, unplumbed, unplumable, with not one drop of evil within it – not one drop of Sin or Suffering or of the possibility of either'.

For indeed dreary and petty, oppressive and imprisoning, is our poor little life, on its surface and apart from God and from His merciful condescensions towards us. But we would not know our misery, we would not feel it as such, were there not Saints and Heroes around us, and Christ our Lord above us, and encompassing all and penetrating all, God – not a Sufferer, but indeed the Sympathiser, God, Joy, the Ocean of Joy, our Home.

A Sermon

preached in Winchester Cathedral on 13 May 1982 when Benedictine vespers were sung by the monks of Farnborough Abbey, and the Cathedral Choir rendered Bruckner's anthem 'Ecce Sacerdos Magnus'. The service was in commemoration of the projected visit to Britain of Pope John-Paul II, but at the time the visit was in the balance, owing to the Falklands war.

Psalm 90.1   Lord thou hast been our refuge; in every generation.
John 14.2   In my Father's house are many mansions.

The hoped-for visit may not materialize, the world is in ever-increasing danger, the unity of the churches may yet be long delayed, but tonight within these ancient, hallowed walls we may for a time be at peace in the worship of God.

> Be thankful thou! for though unholy deeds
> Ravage the world, tranquillity is here.

May this be as the room in which the disciples heard Christ's promise: Peace I leave with you! My peace I give unto you. Not as the world giveth, give I unto you. They represented in all its failures, conflicts, fears, 'the ecclesia at large'; but Jesus said: Let not your heart be troubled ...

I would in these solemn and privileged moments remember as in private duty bound, a Methodist minister of my youth, a Catholic in faith and practice, with some gift of poetry and prayer. He never married; like not a few of those days, he had to devote himself to the care of his mother and spinster sister. He must have been lonely at times. Only as my own ministry has run its course have I come to learn how much he must have suffered in his. 'The way of the high churchman in Methodism is hard,' he once said to me.

It was he who forty years ago introduced me to the Elgar/Newman oratorio *The Dream of Gerontius*. He would sing the angel's Alleluia before his early eucharist at Easter. And I want to use that work in illustration of my theme.

What became the libretto was written by John Henry Newman in 1865. It describes what for Roman Catholic faith is the culminating drama of every human soul – death, judgment, salvation yet through purgatory. A friend once suggested to Alec Robertson that it was called the *dream* of Gerontius because of some lines in the original poem:

> Thou art wrapped and swathed about in dreams,
> Dreams that are true yet enigmatical,
> For the belongings of thy present state,
> Save through such symbols, come not home to thee.

'In other words the experiences of Gerontius are real, but they are like a dream because he does not perceive them through his bodily senses.' Newman's work was as popular as anything he wrote in his lifetime but it is Elgar's music, ten years after Newman's death, which transforms it into greatness. Basil Willey, sometime Professor of English Literature at Cambridge, and a Methodist, said that Newman's poetry and Elgar's music had always tempted and almost persuaded him to accept the doctrine of purgatory.

Which raises a question. Falsehood does not become truth when set to music? Surely if we flirt with that idea, we are being lured by siren voices to spiritual disaster. Art is not a magic which dispenses us from intellectual and moral rigour. The devil may be an artist too. There is music which is undoubtedly great and yet capable of inspiring the deeds of darkness. Wagner and the Nazis is a case in point; and Elgar has some affinities with the composer whom Auden called 'the greatest of the monsters'. And the music of Gerontius is not in the church tradition; very different from some that we have been hearing tonight. There are harmonies and chromatic sequences more daring then than now. My own belief is this – if a theme is capable of being used by an artistic genius which, like Elgar's in this case, seeks the greater glory of God, then art makes possible a transcendence of literalness and of narrow, prosaic understanding, and confronts us with the truth which is present in what may sometimes have been exploited in heresy or made to serve error. It is carried into the eternal order where only truth abides. There is an analogy with this service tonight, which makes us experience a unity which is part of the reality of God and of his will and yet which defeats ecclesiastical negotiation or expression in agreed statements, or even the utterances of a supreme Pontiff.

Consider just three moments in *The Dream of Gerontius* and enter into the magnificence of its conception.

1. Gerontius has reached the moment of death. Terror and dismay come upon him as on our Lord in the garden; in weariness he seeks to commit himself to God. Around his bed are the priest and some of his friends; and they sing 'Profiscere anima Christiana, de hoc mundo' – 'Go forth upon thy journey Christian soul'.

There is the wonder of the church. Weak, mortal, desolate, seemingly mocked by the fate which enables us to think God's thoughts after him, and then after all our struggles, endeavours, temporary achievements, casts us off into painful oblivion, we are not alone and without hope. We may leave this world with all the armies of the divine love and victory. The royal banners go before us; we – even the feeblest of us – have saints apostles, prophets, martyrs for company. And Christ 'leads us through no darker rooms than he went through before'. This is what it means to believe in the Holy Catholic Church and the communion of saints. It is not a matter of what is decreed by canon law or constitutional practices and discipline, important as these are for equity and order on earth; nor is it what may be achieved by reports on authority or ministry or sacraments, necessary as it is that we should know where our obedience is due and be assured that what we receive is authentically of Christ. The true church is the beloved community of those who help each other and lead each other to God in life and death and who do so remembering Jesus. And this is a supernatural fellowship in that its bonds are not only sight and hand but prayer and it includes those no longer on earth, and spiritual powers also. It is not simply a team or a group mind, if there is such a thing. Newman himself was not a convivial person. He would not have been at home in a Methodist class meeting, and would have distrusted group dynamics. Owen Chadwick has said of him that he had a knife inside his mind but was better conversed with on paper. 'If you went to visit him in the Oratory in Birmingham he would have stood on one leg before the hearth and said little worth hearing or more probably nothing.' He once preached in his Anglican days an anti-Methodist sermon, 'Religious worship the remedy for Excitements'. But he lived in the fellowship of a few kindred minds and of angels and archangels and all the company of heaven. And the Holy Catholic Church is a spiritual communion, the succour and support of those who because of it may be never less alone than when alone, in which our individuality is both fulfilled and transcended, our hurts healed and our mortal passage made secure in Christ and those who are his. 'Go forth upon thy journey Christian soul'.

2. Secondly, Gerontius has died, his body is laid in earth, but his soul is borne by his guardian angel towards the throne of God. He is among the saved and the music has unearthly beauty. As he ascends, there are heard the thwarted cackles of the contemptuous and defeated demons, but also the sounds of the heavenly choir, which grow more distinct and louder until in what is surely one of the greatest moments in all artistic and religious experience, almost unbearable, the gates of heaven are opened and the angelic host thunders forth 'Praise to the holiest in the height!' And then Gerontius is given one glimpse of the divine splendour, of God, the Judge of all. And he cannot bear it. 'Take me away,' he cries.

> Take me away and in the lowest deep
>   There let me be
> And there in hope the lone night watches keep
>   Told out for me
> There motionless and happy in my pain,
>   Lone, not forlorn
> There will I sing my sad, perpetual strain
>   Until the morn.

The sight of God, the life of man, is also his death. Now, far more than when hag-ridden by the guilt which Christ's blood has cancelled and Christ's church absolves, does he see himself in all his creaturely unworthiness. This is not the sinner's cringing fear. It is awareness of the infinite qualitative distance between God and the redeemed.

It is not always realized that this is central to Cranmer's unique and much maligned Order of Holy Communion of 1552. At the Sursum Corda, the veil is rent. We behold the heavenly joys. We share in the music with the angels and the saints in light.

> Holy, holy, holy, Lord God of hosts
> Heaven and earth are full of thy glory
> Glory be to thee O Lord most high!

And then, down on our knees. 'We do not presume to come to this thy table, O merciful Lord, trusting in our own righteousness, but in thy manifold and great mercies.'

It is, of course, Isaiah's response in the temple. When he hears the seraphim and sees the King, he does not say 'How glad I am to be here; how happy to be saved', but 'Woe is me!' And this is Catholic and Protestant experience alike.

> O how shall I, whose native sphere
>   Is dark, whose mind is dim,
> Before the ineffable appear
>   And on my naked spirit bear
> The uncreated beam?

And it is this, not simply a sense of sin, or even of alienation, but our humanity, our creatureliness ('I am involved in all mankind'), which makes us forever penitent, and purgatory not old hell writ small, but our only refuge.

3. And this is why purgatory is of the divine mercy, where indeed mercy and judgment are one, its cleansing fires all love. 'Rational and charitable, though unscriptural,' said Basil Willey of the doctrine. And, God knows, it has been an instrument of Christianity at its worst, symbolizing the tyranny, superstitition, commercialism, oppression, corruption of the church unreformed. And yet there is within it charity and hope. The grace of God will make us fit for his presence, partakers of the divine nature, to be one with him in

the company of heaven. And he will not do this by magic, by a Greek metamorphosis, in an instant – we are not made perfect at a clap, said Bunyan. He will do it through a process of education, which enlists the co-operation of my own so feeble will, intelligence and love. There will be pain in it, even frustration at times, but all is of grace and on the morrow there is joy unspeakable and full of glory.

It is the *dream* of Gerontius, as we said. And what is successive in the Oratorio, may be simultaneous in experience, and what is there deferred until after death may be true of the dying life, which is our existence here below. We who may have glimpsed the majesty of God, in whom is our only joy and salvation, should think of this world as a kind of purgatory – for Christians, the intermediate state between the 'now' and the 'not yet', 'a vale of soul making', in which, abandoned to the divine providence, we believe that each sorrow, though not to be desired, may be to our good, even our griefs and pains the chastisement of our peace. Here, we are in a mansion of our Father's house. This earth is no derelict outpost of creation, but although a purgatory, that part of heaven where our lot is cast. And the God whose face we cannot bear to see, shows to us as to Moses, his back, that we may follow him in Christ to the place he has prepared, and where, after God knows what journeyings of the soul, we shall surely arrive.

In *The Dream of Gerontius*, the souls in purgatory sing that 'lofty and melancholy psalm', which Hampden's soldiers sang as they bore his body to the grave, and which Isaac Watts has made a part of English history in his paraphrase, 'Man Frail and God Eternal – Our God our help in ages past'. That hymn may have been once more in our minds these past fearsome weeks. What its associations and those of the psalm signify is that although we are solitary individuals before God, we cannot attain our salvation apart from the whole body of mankind, past, present and to come. And if we seek our own refuge in the mansion of the Father's house prepared for us, we must never forget that his is a house of prayer for all nations, and that our purgation and our prayer are not for ourselves only, but that all the scattered children of God may find in him their eternal home.

Sources, Acknowledgments, Further Reading

The most recent full life of Newman is by Meriol Trevor in two volumes (Macmillan 1962), though there is room for a psychological study. Owen Chadwick, *Newman* (OUP 1983), is a masterly elucidation in a short compass. I am especially indebted to this, to Hilda Graef's *God and Myself: The Spirituality of John Henry Newman* (Peter Davies 1967), though I would gently dispute one or two assumptions, to Robin C. Selby, *The Principle of Reserve in the Writings of John Henry Cardinal Newman* (OUP 1975), and to Andrew Louth, *Discerning the Mystery: An Essay on the Nature of Theology* (Clarendon Press 1983), a book worthy of the most serious discussion, which *inter alia* points the direction for Tractarian theology today. There is a most remarkable lecture on Newman delivered in 1913, by the Baptist scholar, Henry Wheeler Robinson, found in Ernest A. Payne's memoir (Nisbet 1946) pp. 110ff. This contrasts most favourably with the insensitive studies of the Wesleyan, J. H. Rigg, in *Oxford High Anglicanism* (second edition 1899), though these are tempered with occasional, not grudging admiration. Newman's Letters are still being published in massive volumes, now by OUP. There is a small selection, *A Packet of Letters*, edited by Joyce Sugg (OUP 1983). For the spirituality of the 'Second Journey', see the article by Gerald O'Collins in *A Dictionary of Christian Spirituality* (SCM Press 1983).

On the Oxford Movement, there is Owen Chadwick's anthology *The Mind of the Oxford Movement* (A. & C. Black 1960) with a superb introduction, and Geoffrey Rowell, *The Vision Glorious* (OUP 1983). R. W. Church's *The Oxford Movement* (1895 and 1970) is a classic. Yngve Brilioth's *The Anglican Revival* (1925 and 1933) is a fine study by a Lutheran.

'A Sense of Providence' is the title of the last chapter of Owen Chadwick's Gifford Lectures, *The Secularisation of the European Mind* (CUP 1975); it has been borrowed for a short piece by Karl Britton in *The Cambridge Review*, 20 November 1981. Both of these pervade pp. 4–7. On the subject of *Providence* there is a recent book by M. J. Langford (SCM Press 1981) and an article by the same author in *A Dictionary of Christian Spirituality*. Peter Baelz, *Prayer and Providence* (SCM Press 1968) is invaluable, and so is E. Gordon Rupp's vivid and inspiring *Principalities and Powers* (Epworth

Press 1952) – under the shadow of World War II and its post-war period, but still with much of relevance.

Chapter 1

p. 5   William Law, *A Serious Call to a Devout and Holy Life* (Everyman 1906 edn), p. 318.
On mirrors etc. see Lionel Trilling, *Sincerity and Authenticity* (OUP 1972), pp. 24–5, who quotes in a footnote what I cite on p. 5 from Christopher Hill, *The Century of Revolution* (Nelson 1961), p. 253.

p. 7   J. H. Newman, *Letters and Diaries*, xxiii, p. 260.
Karl Britton, art. cit.

pp. 8–9   J. H. Newman, *Parochial and Plain Sermons*, vi, 240–1, also quoted by E. G. Rupp, op. cit., pp. 63–4.

p. 11   J. H. Newman, *Parochial and Plain Sermons*, vi, 113.

Chapter 2

pp. 15–16   Owen Chadwick, *Newman*, p. 11.

p. 16   For a comparison between St John of the Cross and Martin Luther, see Rowan Williams, *The Wound of Knowledge* (Darton, Longman and Todd 1979), chapter 7.

p. 17   For Thomas Traherne see *Centuries of Meditations*, and chapter 4 of C. J. Stranks, *Anglican Devotion* (SCM Press 1961).
For C. E. Raven see *A Wanderer's Way* (Hopkins 1928) and F. W. Dillistone's biography (Hodder and Stoughton 1975).

p. 19   For the Cambridge Platonists see C. A. Patrides' anthology (CUP 1970).

p. 20   The historian referred to is Lawrence Stone and the references are to *The Past and the Present* (Routledge and Kegan Paul 1981), pp. 173–4.

p. 21   Isaac Williams is quoted from his *Tracts 80* and *87* on Reserve. There are extracts from the latter in Elisabeth Jay (ed), *The Evangelical and Oxford Movements* (CUP 1983).

p. 22   J. H. Newman, Letter to James Stephen quoted in R. C. Selby, op. cit., p. 24.

Throughout this section I am much indebted to Andrew Louth's *Discerning the Mystery* from which the sub-title is taken. The final paragraph is a summary with a quotation from p. 147. He also uses a valuable distinction between mystery and problem, found in Gabriel Marcel, *Being and Having* (Fontana 1965), p. 121.

Chapter 3

For this see Isaac Williams, *Tracts*, and also R. C. Selby, op. cit.

p. 29   J. H. Newman, *Parochial and Plain Sermons*, lv, 243. Cf. Luther.

p. 31   Cf. Sir Thomas Browne, *Religio Medici* (*Selected Writings*, ed Geoffrey Keynes, Faber 1968, p. 49): I finde in my confirmed age the sinnes I discovered in my youth; I committed many then because I was a child, and because I commit them still I am yet an infant. Therefore I perceive a man may bee twice a child before the dayes of dotage, and stand in need of Aesons bath before threescore.

p. 33f. Cf. E. G. Rupp, op. cit., p. 26: 'We cannot change the past. But we can change the meaning of the past.' Gabriel Marcel, however, *Being and Having*, pp. 139–40, contends 'that the belief in an immovable past is due to an optical error of the spirit'. People will say 'the past taken in itself does not move; what changes is our way of thinking about it'. But must we not be idealists here and say that the past cannot be separated from consideration of the past? They will say again, 'It is an immutable fact that Peter accomplished an action at such a moment of time. Only the interpretation of the action can vary, and that is exterior to the reality of Peter's action or of Peter himself.' But I do in fact suspect that this last assertion is untrue, though I cannot absolutely prove it so. It seems to me that Peter's reality – infinitely transcendent over Peter's action – remains involved in the interpretation which renews and recreates the action.

p. 33   E. M. Forster, *Two Cheers for Democracy* (Penguin Books 1965), p. 228.

Chapter 4

p. 37   E. B. Pusey, *Sermons during the Season from Advent to Whitsuntide*, p. 212.
           J. H. Newman, *Parochial and Plain Sermons*, v, 259.

p. 38   Newman's interest in the Differential Calculus, quite apart from his theology, may have made him question the whole notion of assurance. 'In truth we arrive at truth by approximations,' he says in a letter to Samuel Wilberforce. This is analogous to the method of the Differential Calculus. See Selby, op. cit., chapter 4 – 'Economy as a Means towards Certainty'.

p. 38f.   W. G. Ward, *Life of Newman*, I, p. 118. Cf. Wheeler Robinson in Ernest A. Payne, op. cit.

pp. 39ff. The latest treatment of angels is by Wesley Carr, *Angels and Principalities* (CUP 1981). See also his article in *A Dictionary of Christian Spirituality*.

p. 42   See John Climacus, *The Ladder of Divine Ascent* (Classics of Western Spirituality, SPCK 1983).

p. 44   I am greatly indebted here to a book which I regard as among the outstanding works of English spirituality: Austin Farrer, *Lord I Believe: Suggestions for turning the Creed into Prayer* (Faith Press 1958), particularly in this instance chapter IV. The quotation comes from p. 34. There is also an echo of F. J. A. Hort, *The Way, the Truth, the Life* (Macmillan second edn 1897), p. 14, the whole of which has influenced me profoundly over the years.

Chapter 5

p. 49   J. H. Newman, *University Sermons* (SPCK 1970), p. 313.
pp. 51–2   J. H. Newman, *Parochial and Plain Sermons*, iv, 243.
p. 52   J. H. Newman, op. cit., iii, 385.
p. 53   Cf. Hilda Graef, *God and Myself*, p. 106.
           Cf. A. Schmemann, *The World As Sacrament* (Darton, Longman and Todd 1966), chapter 2.
p. 54   The quotation is from Andrew Louth, *Discerning the Mystery*, p. 89. Here, I am greatly indebted to a paper read to the Oxford Society for the Study of Historical Theology by Professor

David Martin on 9 June 1983 and to the subsequent discussion, particularly his own further contributions.

p. 55   J. H. Newman, *Parochial and Plain Sermons*, v, 271. For the whole section see Helen Oppenheimer, *The Hope of Happiness* (SCM Press 1983). The last chapter 'Glibness, Gloom and Glory' is particularly germaine.

p. 57   The most recent edition of Julian of Norwich, *Showings*, is in the Classics of Western Spirituality, SPCK 1978.

Cf. Gordon Rupp, 'A Devotion of Rapture in English Puritanism' in R. Buick Knox (ed), *Reformation, Conformity and Dissent* (Epworth Press 1977), pp. 115ff.

Peter Sterry, *Discourse of the Freedom of the Will*, 1675.

pp. 57–9   Friedrich von Hügel, *Essays and Addresses on the Philosophy of Religion*, Second Series (reprinted Dent 1939), pp. 167–213.

A Sermon

For Elgar and *The Dream of Gerontius* see Michael Kennedy, *Portrait of Elgar* (Oxford, 2nd edn 1982), pp. 105–39. Basil Willey's autobiography is *Spots of Time* (Chatto and Windus).